HUMAN RIGHTS

THE THEME OF OUR

TIMES

BY: DR. CLAUDIO F. BENEDI

HUMAN RIGHTS
The Theme of Our Times

Published by I.C. Art
Printed in the United States of America
by BookCrafters

BENEDI DOCTRINE

INSTITUTIONAL VIOLATION

IN ITS DUAL DIMENSION

A) INSTITUTIONAL

B) HUMAN

INTRODUCTION TO THE

INSTITUTIONAL STRUCTURE

OF HUMAN RIGHTS

HUMAN RIGHTS: THE THEME OF OUR TIMES

Human Rights are THE THEME OF OUR TIME, and this is an exceptional moment to attain their enforcement, guardianship, security and protection, precisely in view of the violation of those rights in its dual dimension:

THE INSTITUTIONAL VIOLATION, and

THE HUMAN VIOLATION.

These violations are not only rampant in the Americas, in Cuba, but also in other continents, hence their importance and actuality.

The issue that holds a priority position in the present affairs of the world is, undoubtedly, that of human rights, in which there converge ethics, morals, theology, philosophy, law, sociology and politics, and of which there is talk by statesmen, intellectuals, academicians, politicians and persons who, even without understanding their meaning, proclaim it as a dogma.

We must ask ourselves: "What are human rights?" and vis-à-vis that we must consider two basic aspects of human rights in order to better understand their meaning and application.

First of all: Why must they be established? Can and must human rights be established? What importance does that foundation have?

Second: The violation of human rights in its dual dimension:

A) INSTITUTIONAL VIOLATION

B) HUMAN VIOLATION

Besides, we must analyze them in their national scope, in their internationalization and in their universality, as well as try to answer some basic questions:

How do they originate?

Can they be established, or be declared, or both?

And we must analyze them in three fields or aspects of contemporary thought about the origin of human rights, as well as their behavior in the framework of the various cultures and religions.

A) The ethical-religious: The human being as a person, the IMAGO DEI.
B) The positivist, rationalist.
C) The Socialist-Marxist-Leninist.

1. The ethical-religous position maintains that human rights can and must be established, if we believe that the human person has been created by God, IMAGO DEI, whose concept is comprised within and inseparable from the human nature, lest we leave the human person at the mercy of the changing human rationality and of the ideologies, and exposing it to its limitation, capiti diminutio, and even to its suppression. It is not opposed to their declaration and regulation; all to the contrary, it advocates and wishes it.

2. The positivist and rationalist positions, which maintains that human rights arise from reason of human beings and that they can only be stated, regulated, even established, but not GRANTED BY GOD.

The fact that even without being established, human rights are respected and protected, is a great step forward, but changing, limited and susceptible of being violated, without any fear of the transcendental, to what it means to diminish or destroy that which has been created by God.

3. The socialist-marxist-leninist position, that places the state with all rights and the human person helpless vis-à-vis the state, be it a limited state or a totalitarian state, with which human rights are violated in their dual dimension: **Institutional Violation** and **Human Violation.** This last position denies that human rights come from God; they deny the human person as IMAGO DEI, created in the image and likeness of God.

We cannot analyze in their full extension, as it would be desirable, the implications of all these schools of thought in the conjunction of human rights, but we must analyze, albeit briefly, their scopes of application and their juridicial scope, within the institutional and human framework, and their implications for Law, Theology, Philosophy, Sociology, History and Modern Pedagogy.

There has been a greater advancement after World War II than in the past, both in the declarative sphere and in the normative sphere of human rights.

The President of the United States of America, in his speech before the United Nations General Assembly on September 27, 1993, said: "Let us work with new energy to protect the world's people from torture and repression. As Secretary Christopher stressed at the recent Vienna Conference, human rights are not something conditional, bounded by culture, but rather something universal, granted by God."

THE BENEDI DOCTRINE AND THE COMMUNIST SYSTEM

IN THE BENEDI DOCTRINE IT IS UNDOUBTEDLY
DEMONSTRATED WHY THE COMMUNIST SYSTEM CANNOT BE
REFORMED NOR CHANGED: IT MUST BE ELIMINATED,
BECAUSE IT RUNS COUNTER TO MEN AND WOMEN AS HUMAN
BEINGS, AS A CATEGORY, TO THEIR DIGNITY AND THEIR
FREEDOM.

REGRESSIVE TRANSCULTURATION

THE PROCESS OF REGRESSIVE TRANSCULTURATION COULD ATTAIN THE DESTRUCTION OF THE TRADITION, HISTORY, CULTURE, ETHICS, FAMILY MORALS AND IDIOSYNCRASY OF THOSE NATIONS AND INDIVIDUALS THAT HAVE SUFFERED IT, THROUGH THE SUPERIMPOSITION, ENFORCED BY ARMS, FORCE, TERROR AND FEAR, OR "VALUES AND PRINCIPLES" ALIEN AND FOREIGN TO THE FORMER, DESTROYING THE VALUES AND PRINCIPLES OF THE CIVILIZATION THAT THE WORLD HAD ACHIEVED IN A LONG AND FRUITFUL PROCESS. THE "NATIONAL SOUL" OF THE COUNTRY/PEOPLE WAS DESTROYED; THE STRUCTURE OF THEIR THOUGHTS WAS DISTORTED, AND DEEP TRACKS, AS WELL AS INDELIBLE SCARS HAVE REMAINED IN THE HEARTS OF THE MEN AND WOMEN, LEAVING THEM SUBMERGED IN AN EXISTENTIAL ANGUISH WITHOUT ANY TRANSCENDENTAL SENSE ABOVE THE SPIRITUAL, ETHICAL AND MORAL RUINS LEFT BY MARXISM-LENINISM AND BASED UPON THE TRAGIC "GOSPEL OF HATE." IT IS NECESSARY TO REBUILD, WITH LOVE AND BROTHERHOOD, A WORLD OF PEACE AND FRATERNITY ON EARTH. WE CAN NOT PERMIT THAT THE COLD WAR BE SUBSTITUTED BY A CULTURAL WAR.

T R I B U T E

TO ALL THOSE PERSONS WHOSE HUMAN RIGHTS HAVE
BEEN VIOLATED UPON IN THEIR TWO DIMENSIONS:
INSTITUTIONAL VIOLATION AND HUMAN VIOLATION:
TO THE JEWISH HOLOCAUST, ITS SIX MILLION
VICTIMS OF ADOLF HITLER'S RAGE, WHOSE
SACRIFICE MUST NOT BE IN VAIN, SO HUMANITY
SHALL NOT WITNESS A GENOCIDE AGAIN; TO THE
MILLIONS WHO WERE MURDERED BY STALIN AND THE
SOVIET COMMUNIST MACHINE IN THE SOVIET UNION
AND BY COMMUNIST THROUGHOUT THE WORLD;
AND ESPECIALLY, TO THOSE WHO ARE VICTIMS IN
CUBA, IN PRISONS AND OUTSIDE OF THEM, SINCE
THE WHOLE ISLAND IS A PRISON, DUE TO THE
ANTHROPOCENTRIC COSMOVISION OF TROPICAL
MARXISM-LENINISM.

D E D I C A T I O N

To my father, Mr. Claudio Benedi Rovira

To my mother, Mrs. Concepcion Berruff Garrido

To my wife, Gladys G. Benedi

To my children, Gladys Margarita, Claudio Antonio,
                              Alberto Jorge, Antonio and Hector Joaquin

To my grandchildren, son and daughters in law

My family has been a spiritual and material support for the
completion of this book.

G R A T I T U D E

To my son, Hector Joaquin, to whose perseverance, encouragement, dedication and contribution I finally owe the publication of this book in English.

To my son, Claudio Antonio, whose collaboration and reviewing of the text has contributed to the realization of this work.

To my daughter, Gladys Margarita, without whose coordination and typing work this book could not have been finished on time.

To Jose G. Roig, who has been in charge of translating this work into English. (He is a translator qualified by the U.S. Department of State).

PROLOGUE

PROLOGUE

by

Dr. Guillermo J. Jorge

I

The book that we are going to preface is a monography about "human rights." The issue studied on same is fundamental and has an enormous transcendence for the evaluation of the priorities in the institutions of humanism and democracy in our time.

These institutions of human rights, with a centuries long tradition in the Judeo-Christian civilization, have never been more in force than now, at the end of this millennium.

With a history that dates back to the "Magna Carta" of England (1215), the "Bill of Rights" of 1869, The "Declaration of Independence" of the United States (July 4, 1776) and the "Declaration of the Rights of Man and of the Citizen," adopted by the French Revolution on August 26, 1789, Dr. Benedi goes beyond that immediate background and studies the statements of Father Bartholome de las Casas, who in his "Most Brief Account of the Destruction of the Indies" (1552) thundered against violations of the human rights of the aborigenes of the New World.

Upon digging even deeper into this background, the author of this book analyzes the work and the ideas of the rightly called "Father of International Law," Father Francisco de Vitoria, who in his book "Indis et de Jure Belli Relectiones" (1526) gives us the first modern definition of international law based upon natural law, upon stating: "Quo naturalis ratio inter omnes gentes constituit."

Dr. Benedi finishes that historical introduction by performing a study of the contributions of the Cuban priest, Father Felix Varela, to the doctrine of liberty and human rights, as a valuable and always present background of the institution under study in this work.

II

If we make an abstraction of that background and face the interest that human rights have aroused in the present generations, it appears that these rights were "invented" yesterday, because at no other time as in the last fifty years have they been raised as a shield and a doctrine to preserve the dignity of human beings in all nations, in all latitudes of the planet, with no distinction as to race, social class or political affiliation.

Perhaps this is so because never before had humankind endured tyrannies so terribly inhuman as those of Hitler's and Stalin's, as well as others that are sad to remember.

Should any doubt linger about the latter, the trials of Nuremberg, after World War II, and the denouncements against Stalin brought about by Krushchev before the XX Congress of the Soviet Communist Party, revealed the magnitude of the holocaust suffered by Jews in Europe and the extermination of large masses of the Russian people at the hands of Stalin.

After Krushchev's report, a table of values was devised in the Soviet Union to evaluate crimes against innocent citizens, violence against the mass-murdered members of the military and all procedures experienced under the Stalinist regime, that had remained hidden but that, when confirmed in their tragic and evident truthfulness, threw a shroud of dishonor upon communism.

In this struggle for human rights during this century, it must be said that in Cuba, that has endured thirty years of Castro-communist totalitarianism, in which all human rights have been denied and limited to the hilt, the constant, permanent and fruitful work of Dr. Benedi stands out, inside and outside of all international fora.

III

A pioneer in that struggle, he has been the main gladiator in that fight and men and women who owe him their lives, their freedom and their personal integrity are counted by the hundreds.

The personality of Dr. Benedi is thus invested with an international projection that consecrates him as the most outstanding in this environment of "human rights" and nobody is, because of that, more deserving of the "Nobel Peace Prize" than he, given his noble quality and indisputable merits. It is possible that such an award may never be given him, but should he be honored with it any time, nobody could say that the awarding of the prize was not fully warranted. Otherwise, I know that for Dr. Benedi it is enough to know, in order to live with pride, that he has known how to fulfill his duty upon placing his intellect and will at the service of those noble causes.

For Dr. Benedi, the writing of this book has been easy, despite having attained with it a work of profound analysis and great transcendence in Political Law; since the same is, simply, the summation of all works that as reports and juridical briefs he has produced before the various International Organizations through a quarter of a century. But if that was easy, this has been very difficult, since it is necessary to consider that he had to overcome many obstacles at the beginning in order to obtain that his arguments would be successful towards the vindication of human rights.

This work that begins, as we have said, with a study about the background of human rights, performs a detailed and meticulous incursion through Constitutional Law, Public and Private International Law, to arrive later at the study, in an analytical manner, of the Reports and Agreements of the International Commission and of the Inter-American Commission for Human Rights; it likewise studies the violations of those rights in the Soviet Union and Cuba, and ends with a series of annexes that add a great value as a reference work. But perhaps the most significant aspect of all the text of this book, because of its originality and present actuality, is the exhibition of the "institutional violation of human rights," the so called "Benedi Doctrine," already recognized under that name in all international fora and by the current President of the United States, the Congress of the United States and the Inter-American Commission on Human Rights.

IV

Dr. Benedi and I were classmates at the University of La Habana, we graduated as attorneys together, I have known the author of this book for many years. Throughout that wide path I have seen Dr. Benedi, who has been his own sculptor, polish the edges of his personality as a jurist and attorney for noble causes, in order to build an image and likeness of the Creator. With this work, that is a summation of his constant efforts, Claudio

Benedi has performed a work as St. Ignatius of Loyola wished: "To the greatest glory of God" and of the dignity of the human person.

In consideration of that work,   in the consecration of his great achievements in the political and academic fields,   the author of this prologue dedicated the following verse to the friend and illustrious companion:

V

"THE BENEDI DOCTRINE"

To Dr. Claudio Benedi
Defender of human rights.

Defender of human rights. Invincible gladiator!
In your trench, claiming for justice for your brethren,
You have converted the FATHERLAND into a flag.

How many beautiful pages are accumulated
In order to sing a hymn to your crusade
In constant struggle, where the glories
Of a betrayed FATHERLAND are emulated?

Tomorrow, your doctrine shall be a shelter
It shall be a beacon of light, very resplendent,
A rainbow, that as an immense ring,
Will protect with justice the penitent.

And when the Academies of the Law
Will devote themselves to study their history,
The "Benedi Doctrine" shall be already a deed,
Recorded on the credit to your memory.

Miami, January 10, 1988.
Dr. Guillermo J. Jorge

TABLE OF CONTENTS

ANNEXES

A) Bill of Rights of the United States of America, December 15, 1791

B) American Declaration of the Rights and Duties of Man, Inter-American System, signed in Columbia on April, 1948.

C) Universal Declaration of Human Rights, United Nations, signed December 10, 1948.

D) European Convention on Human Rights, Rome, 1950

E) Declaration of The Rights of The Child, United Nations, November 20, 1959.

F) American Convention on Human Rights, signed 1969

G) Helsinki Conference (Human Rights Section) signed 1975

THE "BENEDI DOCTRINE"

The "Benedi Doctrine" is based upon the full dignity of men and women, on their freedom and on all of their human attributes, that are inherent and intrinsic to the human person, as a category, made in the Creator's image, whose inalienable and imprescriptible rights are outside of the jurisdiction of any earthly authority, which shall not be able to limit, reduce, violate or surpress them.

Man and woman are as a category in themselves, created by God, made up by body and soul as a unit, who participate in the divine and transcendental towards God, and in the human, with all of their attributes and rights.

When in the constitution and or the laws of a country there is an attempt to legalize slavery of a human being, we are in the presence of an Institutional Violation of human rights.

When in the constitution and or the laws of a country there is an attempt to deprive, limit, or surpress women's right to vote, we are in the presence of an Institutional Violation of human rights.

When in the constitution and or the laws a state assumes all the powers and all the rights, and the human person is deprived of rights, and is defenseless against the state, we are in the presence of an Institutional Violation of human rights.

When a state surpresses the right to own private property, we are in the presence of an Institutional Violation of human rights. The state can limit and condition the right to own private property for the common good previously established, with all the guarantees of human rights and moral and natural laws, but it can never surpress it.

When a violation is committed against what man represents in his dignity, his freedom, his inalienable and imprescriptible rights, we are witnessing and Institutional Violation, that has two dimensions:

> *The Institutional Violation in the Constitution and the Laws, as a result of a system which is totally incompatible with men and women in their capacities as*

human persons, and the violation in its Human Dimension, that can be committed in a totalitarian manner, as a product of the system itself, or autocratically, because of the abuse of power; the latter can be corrected because it does not affect the system nor is it derived from it, but rather from the undue use of power.

The Institutional Violation is committed in those countries with statist or totalitarian regimes, where the State, represented by the Party, assumes and absorbs all the attributes and rights of the human person, and it is thus stipulated in the laws and all legal regulations in force.

The Human Dimension of the Institutional Violation of Human Rights is committed directly against persons, be it a violation related to male and female political prisoners, or against the whole population of the country submitted to such violations.

These Institutional Violations, in their Human Dimension, can be committed in totalitarian or authoritarian regimes. In totalitarian regimes, these violations are intrinsic to the system.

In authoritarian regimes, that violation is committed through the abuse of power, or the arbitrary use of power. It can be corrected because it is not due to the system. Once the abuse of power is suppressed, the system recovers its normalcy.

The fundamental and basic issue in our times is "THE FULL DIGNITY OF MAN AND WOMAN AS A CATEGORY," that precedes the juridical and political structures and all ideologies. This includes the human person in its primordial creation, in the very origin of the human being, man and woman, as God's creatures, created in His image and likeness and endowed with all divine and human attributes, above any limitative rationality and any casuist and circumstantial interpretation that would not encompass the fullness of their origin. It Transcends all systems and all times, because it is prior to them and cannot be subjected to such rational limitations.

The definition of HUMAN RIGHTS, in itself, does not include the fullness of the human category, because the latter transcends the former; it goes beyond the rational concept of human rights.

God Himself, being Almighty, only limited Himself in the freedom that He gave men and women to choose, with their own will, the road to good or that to evil, the destinies of their lives, that have a transcendental sense. This freedom has been suppressed in some instances: With the INSTITUTIONAL VIOLATION that some ideologies have committed and still commit; in our times, the Marxist-Leninist doctrine, and/or the limited HUMAN VIOLATION, committed totalitarily in the communist regimes, and autocratically in rightist regimes, because of the arbitrary use of power.

We have documented the INSTITUTIONAL VIOLATION for the last 30 (thirty) years, in uncontested documents, with plenty of evidence, recognized both in the Americas and in Europe.

The INSTITUTIONAL VIOLATION is the total destruction of those values and principles enshrined in the Judeo-Christian civilization, and in those other documents such as the American Declaration of the Rights and Duties of Man, which on April 1993 reached 45 years of having been proclaimed by the Ninth International American Conference, held in Bogota, Colombia, in 1948; the Universal Declaration of Human Rights, approved by the United Nations on December 10, 1948; and in the American Convention on Human Rights, and in the juridical and political structure that protects and guarantees those human rights in the world, as well as the Helsinki Agreements, in its section about respect for human rights and fundamental liberties, including those of thought, conscience, religion and beliefs.

The inalienable and imprescriptible rights consecrated by God on behalf of the human person, and which make up its dignity, beyond the human limitations.

This INSTITUTIONAL VIOLATION is, in our times, intrinsic to the Marxist-Leninist system, and it could not survive without those institutional violations, as it has been demonstrated.

By means of this INSTITUTIONAL VIOLATION, the communist regime displaces, destroys and replaces the system of values and principles enshrined in our Western Civilization on behalf of the human person, committing a true crime against humanity, which makes men and women go back to stages already overcome by present civilization in the modern world. It is regressive, anachronistic and backwardly. It constitutes a REGRESSIVE TRANSCULTURATION, with false values that dispossesses men and women of their sacred attributes, juridical, political and social.

3

We are also dealing, nothing more and nothing less that with the destruction of the NATIONAL SOUL of each country, where there is the application of their traditions, their history, their culture and of everything that represents men and women as a category. Upon destroying those values and principles in each person, they are destroying in the country that they belong to, the whole of society.

This is the basic and fundamental confrontation of our time, in the Americas and the World. It is a struggle between two entirely antagonistic and irreconcilable systems, because of their respective values and principles.

We could point out several countries where that philosophical, political, social and theological phenomenon is taking place in our days. In the Americas, unfortunately, we can show that confrontation in Cuba. The replacement of a system by another. Where this is most evident and easily verifiable is in what regards the human person and the violation of his/her rights, of the values and principles that make up our culture.

This is the confrontation between the ANTHROPOCENTRIC COSMOVISION OF MAN AND THE WORLD, AND THE THEOCENTRIC COSMOVISION.

The STATE OF LAW is essential, basic and fundamental for the protection of human rights. Where a regime of law does not exist, there is no protection for human rights.

Where a STATE OF LAW does not exist, the human person is defenseless vis-à-vis the State; he/she is deprived of all appeals that might protect them against the TOTALITARIAN STATE. This is unquestionable.

The basic substratum of the culture and coexistence of the Western World is the full dignity of the human person and of his/her human rights; its theological, philosophical and political viewpoint of freedom, in the widest transcendental and human concept.

This is the basic foundation in our relationships between free states, speaking juridically and politically, and among their own citizens.

This dignity of the human person and these human rights transcend boundaries; they cannot be subjected to the whim of every state, because they make up the most sacred values of our civilization, and without respect and protection for them, we would regress to primitive stages already overcome by our civilization.

Our commitment with human rights is not only of a religious nature, but also political and juridical. It is a tacit and expressed commitment. Consecrated and elliptical, inferred as to human beings. Our relationships among peoples, individuals and states cannot develop upon any other foundation with a larger area. No regime, no ideology is allowed to erect walls in order to violate and negate these rights.

Mankind is an indivisible whole in its human dimension. The interdependency of states must, of necessity, be based upon the unlimited respect for human rights, that distinguishes men and women, precisely because of their dignity.

The struggle of the present world is based upon respect for human rights, upon its enforceability in all latitudes. The human person as a category first, before society, before the State and above them. Because the fullness of the society and the State depends precisely upon the human person, and must be based upon him/her.

Totalitarian regimes, such as Nazism (National-Socialism), Fascism (born under Mussolini in Italy), and Marxism-Leninism in our times, proclaim that the state has all the rights and is the dispenser of gifts for each citizen. We already have a plethora of examples about the monstrosity of this for those peoples that have been unfortunate enough to endure them, and for those others that are still subjected to that anti-natural system, that denies God, enslaves men and women and puts them in such a level of submission as no other ages of mankind knew.

They have been, and still are, a TRAGIC UTOPY, as Pope John Paul II has stated.

We are not dealing, then, with an isolated event, but with a present reality and a potential problem for all of humankind.

The pretext utilized by totalitarianism to deprive human beings of their freedoms and to violate their human rights has been a fallacy that does not admit any adversarial evidence. Nobody, except a dogmatic fanatic of those repressive systems would dare today to proclaim the "goodness" of such a monstrosity against the dignity and freedom of men and women.

In a prison, inmates might want perhaps to have food, clothing and medicines at the price of their dignity and freedom. But the fact remains that in those regimes which proclaim that they have attained such results, nobody has been able to obtain adequate food, clothing or medicines. This is easily verifiable.

There has never been, nor is there any peace within those parameters, as Pope John Paul II has proclaimed: "Peace is born out of the inviolable rights of the human person."

It was also underlined in our Americas by the Mexican patriot, Don Benito Juarez: "Peace is respect for the rights of others."

The human person is endowed with attributes and values that make up his/her dignity. Those are inalienable and imprescriptible. The so called human rights are related to the Gospel more that to Law.

God, albeit being Almighty, as we have demonstrated, limited Himself in the freedom that He gave to the creatures whom he had created in His image and likeness, so they could choose their own destinies, the road to good or to evil.

All of this, which is transcendental, vertical towards God, is what confers men and women, as a category, their human dimension, their full dignity, that precedes all law and all purely human rationalization.

That is why, upon qualifying all the attributes of the human person and his/her dignity within the category of human rights, we have to keep in mind that such a definition is inadequate and does not include the entirety of the human person.

Starting from the acceptance of the qualification of rights, be they natural or juridical, we must enter into the placement of these rights and the consideration given them today.

By nature, all men and women have equal rights and freedoms: Ius naturale .

Human rights are universal and indivisible, intrinsic to the human person as such, own attributes of which they cannot be deprived, neither by deed nor by law.

The human person, as a subject of the law, can only with freely given consent by each individual, delegate the exercise or the regulation of some of these rights, in order to contribute to the fulfillment of the common good, for the enforcement of social solidarity, for national integration, for the peaceful coexistence of a human nucleus of a nation. In the same manner that sovereign states oblige themselves freely in a regional or worldwide interdependency to better accomplish their ends.

Human rights accompany men and women in whatever places they may be, above all frontiers, as human persons: Ius gentium . They are intrinsic to the human nature.

Nobody is empowered to deprive another person of his/her human rights, nor to limit them. The institutional and human violation, in its dual dimension, becomes a crime against humanity.

The "Benedi Doctrine" gave violations of human rights a dual dimension: INSTITUTIONAL VIOLATIONS AND HUMAN VIOLATIONS.

Those who attempt to deprive, or who actually deprive human beings of their freedoms and rights, shall not only be responsible before the laws, before their peoples, before the international organizations in charge of their protection and enforcement, but they shall also be violating sacred rights that God gave us, to each of His creatures, whatever latitude they may have been born at; they would be invading an area that God Himself set as the limit for His power. Human power cannot ever be superior to God's power, nor can the former limit or destroy the freedom He has created for men and women. When in the constitution and or the laws of a country there is a discrimination on the human person for reason of race (such as Apartheid), creed, ideology, social class, or political ideas there in lies an institutional violation of human rights because there is an attempt to limit, condition, or surpress the inalienable and imprescriptible rights of the human person against his/her dignity and liberty.

THE HUMAN PERSON AS A CATEGORY

The classification or CATEGORY (from the Greek, kategoria , attribute, also in an Aristotelian sense), when referring to the human person, man and woman, in their theological, philosophical, juridical, political and social senses, allows us to locate ourselves in an area thus far not totally explored, neither by the political science nor by the political philosophy. It is a very new concept of men and women, that contributes a true revolution by the end of the twentieth century, when it seemed that, on one hand the ideologies (in full sundown at the present time) and on the other hand the collective aspect of our human relations (above the human category, as an individual), were going to drown the human being's longings and hopes to fully develop, which is the only way of being. That is why the "BENEDI DOCTRINE" comes to the rescue of the human person as a category that precedes any rational conception, one with a transcendental and sacred origin, which confers it a dimension thus far not duly categorized.

We say to the human person, man and woman: "You are the issue, here and now; the issue is your DIGNITY, complete, in full, such as God conceived it for you, above human reason. Those rights that you have are sacred and transcend the juridical, philosophical, social, political fields, but cannot be confused there, nor limited or diminished in their essence, but developed, so you shall be able to exercise them fully."

OF HUMAN RIGHTS

For the purposes of this work, we will divide HUMAN RIGHTS into two categories, equal between them and derived from a single source:

A. NATURAL HUMAN RIGHTS

B. CIVIL AND POLITICAL HUMAN RIGHTS

"Natural human rights" would be those which are given to the human person in accordance with his/her dignity, because of being a human person, God given, inalienable and imprescriptible, in accordance with their nature, the have been called "IUS NATURALISTAS" or "IUS NATURALIS." These are rights intrinsic to the human person, inherent to it, born with him/her and which accompany human beings for all of their lives: "Men and women are born free and equal in law, and are endowed to live in freedom."

"Civil and political human rights" will be those which transcend the juridical order, as well as the political and social orders, and ARE ENSHRINED in the constitutions and laws, recognized to the human person because of their being intrinsic to the same.

The interrelation between these human rights cannot be divided into separate sections, nor can distinctions be established among them to limit them or to diminish their exercise. Their integrity is indivisible and imprescriptible.

Jose Marti, The Apostle of Cuban Independence, said "The first law of the Republic of Cuba must be RESPECT FOR THE FULL DIGNITY OF MAN." That is the definition of said concept.

SOME HISTORICAL BACKGROUND ABOUT HUMAN RIGHTS

It is in the United States Revolution where we can find the most clear and solid proclamations of human rights, with a legal strength, that have as their essential foundation the acknowledgment of human rights inherent to the human being, and that the state is obliged to respect and defend.

The long struggle between this acknowledgment and the British statements, especially the Magna Carta from King John in 1215, the Petition of the British Parliament to King Charles I in 1628 and the Declaration of Rights, or "Bill of Rights," demanded by parliament from William and Mary, Princes of Orange, in 1689 in order to climb the throne, whose declaration was approved by the Chamber of Lords and the House of Commons, intended to declare the rights of subjects and to regulate the succession rights.

Let us examine the scope of the Magna Carta and we shall realize that, albeit of a same Anglo-Saxon origin, the Declaration of the United States of America is really the one that completes the projection of what we call human rights presently.

In the Magna Carta, King John promises and commits the throne upon the following guarantees and rights: (a) Limitation of the sovereign's powers and his obligation to consult both the Lords and the Commons, which constitute the parameters of parliamentarism; (b) No taxes shall be imposed without previous consultation and approval from Parliament, and (c) Habeas Corpus, the basic guarantee of individual freedom, the trial by jury and independence of the judiciary or those who impart justice.

The Declaration of Rights from the United States is related more to the Gospel than to the rationalistic conception of society. There exists a substantial difference between them, as we will see.

The "Bill of Rights" for the Commonwealth of Virginia, dated June 12, 1774, two years before the Declaration of Independence of the United States, reads: "Article 1. All men are, by nature, free and independent, have innate rights, such as life, freedom, property and the pursuit of happiness and security, of which they cannot be deprived or limited by any means because of the circumstance of living in a society."

The Declaration of Independence of the United States of America, proclaimed on July 4, 1776, states that "All men have been created equal, that they have been endowed by their Creator with certain inalienable rights" and that among those rights there must be placed in the first slots: Life, liberty and the pursuit of happiness. It emphasizes that, for the guarantee of enjoyment of those rights, men have established governments, the authority of which derives from the consent of the governed.

The first substantial differentiation that we find between the British and North American texts refers to the very origin of those human rights. The United States declares expressly that they emanate from the Creator and are related to the very origin of the human being, while the British texts refer to the people as a collective entity.

Here, in North America, the origin of man in God is underlined, the Creator, and the fact that his rights, besides emanating from God, are intrinsic to each person as a category, as a human being.

The British declaration adequately proclaims the rights of the people, while the United States proclaims the rights of man, and declares that those rights are intrinsic to him/her and that they are above any power, be it legislative or not, since they emanate from a Superior Power, whom man cannot reach, modify or amend.

Life is the first basic right of human beings; without it, the others have no value. Alphonse X, the Wise, said it: "Whoever deprives me of life, deprives me of all my rights."

These refer to freedom, the unlimited freedom that God gave us and the only thing in which God Himself, being Almighty, established a limit for Himself. That freedom gives us the right to choose, perhaps the highest responsibility that men and women have in their lives, because IT GIVES SENSE TO THEIR LIVES AND MAKES THEM MASTERS OF THEIR OWN DESTINIES. The Declaration of Independence of the United States of America adds: "... to guarantee those rights, and their enjoyment, men have established governments among them, whose authority emanates from the consent of the governed."

These declarations, both the British and more especially that of the United states of America, are the first statements about the human rights of the world. Thus, we can point out, doing justice at the same time that we render homage of gratitude to the Founding Fathers of the United States, that it was in this country where the declarative and normative bases were set for the acknowledgment, respect and enforcement of HUMAN RIGHTS in the world, starting from the events listed above.

To underline what we state, we would like to mention a historical event, little know and divulged, albeit it is recognized in History. The Marquis of Lafayette, who had been strongly influenced by the North American Revolution and had participated in its War of Independence, takes with him to France the basic principles of the U.S. Declaration of Independence and requests, in a historical proposal, that the French Revolution will adopt a Declaration of Human Rights similar to that of the United States, and that it will incorporate the same into its Constitution. This takes place on July 11, 1789, that is, thirteen years after the U.S. Declaration of Independence had occurred. Said proposal was adopted by the French Revolution upon request from the Marquis of Lafayette on August 26 of the same year, as a DECLARATION OF THE RIGHTS OF MAN AND THE CITIZEN.

This action sets a landmark in the development of human rights, the acceptance of same within the normative framework of a constitution, and the higher importance that it has for the development of the guarantees for these rights, the acknowledgment of same, respect for them and their incorporation into International Law.

It is a fact of historical importance that there is, in a constitution, the recognition of the existence of human rights inherent to the human person, to his/her dignity, and that these are prior to and higher than the State. An insurmountable limit is being set for the State, that it shall not be able to trespass it; there shall be an express prohibition to exercise it in order to affect, or in any form to limit, and much less to surpress those rights, upon which it does not have, nor has it been given, any jurisdiction whatsoever. There is the human being as a category, higher than and prior to the State, and upon whom the latter has neither power nor jurisdiction to affect his/her rights, the full exercise of those rights and the full development of his/her human dignity.

Here arises one of the most serious problems encountered by Humanity in our time: That which relates to the scope of protection of human rights. Although the Constitution itself recognizes that these human rights are intrinsic to the human person, innate, prior to the state and outside of its limitative jurisdiction, which is unquestionable, however, many of the States are still reluctant to allow an extra- territoriality for those rights, an international jurisdiction to protect them with a sufficient coercive power, instead of leaving them at the mercy of the State within its frontiers.

The Classic School of International Law has been evolving towards a wider scope for the protection of these rights, but in the past, International Law had been reluctant to recognize the functions and rights of the individual per se, not even regarding those human rights that were inherent to his/her dignity.

It was the monstrous holocaust committed by Nazism with the extermination of six million Jews, which shocked the conscience off the civilized world and mobilized countries and their jurisdictional organs to open a wider scope for the protection of the human person as such, in his/her full dignity, above all boundaries, with the protection of International Law and adequate powers so the Jewish Holocaust shall not happen again anywhere in the world. So that the deaths of so many innocent people shall not be in vain, but so that they may be, immolated for us and for all humanity, those to whom we render homage and the acknowledgment of their having been, with their sacrifice, those who placed the human being in its full dignity, as a category that deserve respect, recognition and guarantee of the fact that their human rights, inalienable and imprescriptible, are entitled to, because of their being intrinsic to the human person and derived from the Creator, prior to the State and above all geographic, political, ideological, economical, social frontiers, or those of any kind.

Presbyter Felix Varela, a Cuban, posed in Spain, in the courts of Cadiz in 1823, the following:

> *"When all thing will have been disturbed, and*
> *men, through an accumulation of relationships,*
> *the most embarrassing and unavoidable, will have*
> *come to lose their imprescriptible rights, without*
> *being able to claim them, except at the cost of their*
> *lives; when a few, through forgetting the origin of*
> *their power, will have become the arbiters of the*
> *fate of others, shall we say that this is a happy*
> *people, or rather a conjunction of slaves in whom*
> *disgrace has established its dwelling?"*

We must cite among the pioneers of respect for human rights, Fray Bartolome de las Casas, who in his work entitled "A Very Brief Account of the Destruction of the Indies," published in 1552, condenses the cases and denounces the circumstances under which many violations of the human rights of the indigenous peoples were committed in this hemisphere. He was a true defender of the dignity and the integrity of the human person, in the cases of indigenous peoples. He inspired himself on the Gospel and on the teachings of Father Francisco de Vitoria.

SOVEREIGNTY AND HUMAN RIGHTS

Sovereignty derives from the people; this is an axiom in true democracies, and a basic principle upon which the rights of peoples are based. "National sovereignty" is not only a geographical or territorial issue, it also reaches the field of law.

Thus, power is in sovereignty, and the latter in the people, who is that which must grant and guarantee power.

As Abraham Lincoln said: "Democracy is the government of the people, by the people and for the people."

Each individual is the depositary of that sovereignty. If the people elect their rulers so that they would exercise that sovereignty, the ownership of that sovereignty continues to be in the people, and human rights are included within this ownership.

It would be absurd to believe that people would elect their rulers for them to violate the human rights of the former, which are inalienable and imprescriptible; that is why totalitarian dictatorships and autocratic dictatorships run counter to the full exercise of human rights, but on different levels. The former because of the system itself. These practice the INSTITUTIONAL VIOLATION OF HUMAN RIGHTS IN THEIR CONSTITUTION AND LAWS, and there is also, in various degrees in both, a VIOLATION IN ITS HUMAN DIMENSION; but in autocracies this is not attributable to the system, but to arbitrary use of power, albeit that allows for reform without affecting the system.

If the people have no rights to exert their rights of sovereignty in order to elect their rulers, human rights have been violated.

Benjamin Constant gives us a definition of liberty that could encompass that for all rights. Liberty consists of "practicing that which society has no right to impede." In this definition, there is contrast between human rights and society. The latter cannot impede the exercise of the inalienable and imprescriptible rights of men and women, which are prior to society and the state and upon which they have no jurisdiction. The common good will limit, in some cases, some rights, but in this analysis we are dealing with pointing out that innate human rights cannot be violated nor surpressed in the name of society, let alone on behalf of the state, because they are inherent to the human being. This is one of the basic confrontations of our time: The collision between the individual, the human person, vis-à-vis the state, on which road exploitation of human beings by the state has been reached, the worst of all exploitation's, whereby the state becomes a party, the Communist Party and this, in turn, is controlled by the dictator on duty. Thus, the latter will become "the owner of the lives and properties" and the worst transgressor of human rights that humankind has known, in its dual dimension: INSTITUTIONAL AND HUMAN.

The equilibrium among the human person, society and state is a fundamental issue in our time, and the basis for the full exercise of the rights of men and women and for the development and growth of the society and the effective operation of the state.

Charles Louis de Secondat, universally known as the baron of Montesquieu, defined the freedom of the individual in society with a more juridical sense, when he stated: "It is the right to do everything allowed by law." Maybe he inspired upon the Romans, who left a clearer definition for us upon saying: "Everything that is not forbidden, is allowed," although we would add "by morals, by the laws and within the limits of the exercise of each person's rights."

Whatever is unjust, shall never be just because others would want it to be. A majority cannot get the unjust to become just upon the strength of its majority vote.

No government, whatever its origin may be, has the right of life or death upon the governed, nor can it be the owner of life and property.

Independence, sovereignty and freedom originate and rely upon individual freedom, the guarantee of human rights.

SOCIETY AND HUMAN RIGHTS

Since the dawn of humanity, men and women have sought and they have attained to evidence the necessity of respect for human rights.

As the basic foundation of respect for the human person, we would have to go looking for it in the religious sense of man and woman, in the springing up of religions, mainly the Judeo-Christian civilization that conforms the very foundation of Western civilization, without, for that reason, debasing other religious denominations that have and still have a great deal of influence in large human conglomerates, such as Islam (Monotheist civilization).

If the human being is made in the image and likeness of God, the human person acquires a sacred, transcendental nature, possessing inalienable and imprescriptible rights as we have said above, from which we must start in the civilized organization of our modern societies and nations.

The juridical, political and social structures of our modern societies have, as their foundation, the human person and those rights that emanate from him/her, which transcend International Law.

It would be extensive to enumerate the whole process of systematization and juridicity in the evolution of human rights, laws and national constitutions, as well as in the classic and modern international law, the former being reluctant to consider the individual and his/her rights because of the jealousy of states about their internal jurisdiction and the understood sovereignty, at that time, as an absolute value, and the latter which, after World War II, has been following an accelerated and progressive process in favor of protection of human rights and, with a great flexibility, has been norming human rights in multinational declarations, covenants and agreements that have enhanced increasingly the declarative and normative scope of human rights.

SOME HISTORICAL BACKGROUND

Let us examine this in International Law, in accordance with the Ancient or Classic School.

The rights of persons, "Ius gentium," with the "Communitas gentium," were the basic foundation of the international organic structure. There was then a strong theological influence on International Law, which becomes more evident during the medieval period.

A person whom we could call "the Father of International Law," was he who took this kind of law out of its stagnation and made it pierce the frontiers.

Father Francisco de Vitoria said: "PACTA SUM SERVANDA."
"ONE FREELY AGREES, BUT IS OBLIGED TO THE COVENANT."

This basic foundation of International Law is shown, under the bust of the illustrious priest and jurisconsult, at the Organization of American States, in its seat in Washington, D.C.

The outstanding Dominican, a lifetime professor of the University of Salamanca, in Spain, was he who projected into the present and future the International Law, the rights of person, born of Roman Law.

Since 1526, in his capacity as a Professor of Theology in that university, he developed his concept of International Law, gathering his works and published them in the Indis et de Jure Belli Relectiones, which can be formally considered as the first treaties of that kind in the world.

In that work, Fr. Vitoria lists everything related to the condition of the King and the peculiar situation in the law of the aborigines of the Americas.

Fr. Vitoria gives us there a modern definition of the rights of persons, based upon natural law: "Quo naturalis ratio inter omnes gentes constituit."

He enhances his concept of International Law, overlapping national boundaries and pointing out that from it there emanate rights and duties for all men and women, independently from the national juridical organizations. He thus establishes the universality of rights that are intrinsic to the human person.

"There are things that belong to no one because of the rights of persons," he adds, and then goes on to establish the relationship between the rights of persons and natural law, the former derived from the latter, which is a source of rights and obligations.

Fr. Vitoria establishes a limit for the temporary power of the sovereign, or any other power: "This limit is the rights that every human being has, inherent to his/her nature, inalienable and imprescriptible, and it shapes and projects human rights as a juridical category, aside from the respect and guarantee due it, and the exercise of which is the foundation for civilized coexistence stemming from the human person; from this all other rights will be generated, be they societies or of states." There surges from the brilliant conception of Fr. Vitoria the "Homus Sapiens," a subject of inviolable rights, and it starts to shape the juridical personality of the human being. Although it will take time to recognize the human person as a subject of law, in International Law, because of the jealousy of the states.

Once more, the Americas and their aborigines would play the role, as human beings, of subjects for the law, in order to elaborate general principles that would later serve as a valuable background in the international juridical system for the protection of human rights.

There, in that fountain, as we have said, Fray Bartolome de Las Casas undoubtedly drank the juridical foundation for his defense of the human rights of the aborigines, whose rights were violated by the conquest.

CONSTITUTIONS AND HUMAN RIGHTS

The Political Constitution of the United States, dated September 17, 1787, was the first one to incorporate the principles listed in the Declaration of Independence on July 4, 1776, and later in the Bill of Rights.

The thirteenth Amendment to the Constitution of the United States, in 1865, incorporated the emancipation of the slave, thus completing the constitutional structure for the protection of human rights.

The Marquis of Lafayette, as we have said above, took to France the text of human rights enacted in the United States of America, and they were incorporated there to the Constitution which emanated from the French Revolution, on August 26, 1789, as the Declaration of the Rights of Man and the Citizen.

The first professorship of Constitutional Law established in the Americas was founded by Presbyter Felix Varela at the Seminary of San Carlos, La Habana, Cuba, in 1821. When classes started, 200 hundred students had been enrolled.

When the courts of Cadiz were assembled, Father Varela was elected as the representative from Cuba before that body, to which effect he prepared a study, monumental for its time, entitled: "REMARKS ABOUT THE POLITICAL CONSTITUTION OF THE SPANISH MONARCHY." He was then the Professor of Philosophy and Constitution at the Seminary of San Carlos, above mentioned.

We feel that it is convenient to mention that background in the development of our Constitution and International Law, our contribution to international elaboration of norms.

Father Varela states in the introduction to that work: "The object of these remarks is not to make a comment about the Political Constitution of the Spanish Monarchy, but presenting its foundations, sovereignty, and liberty and the principles that emanate from every constitution, and from this come the division of powers and their attributions. Here is all of the constitutional system."

In this first paragraph of his introduction, Father Varela gives us a definition and a synthesis of what a constitution is and ought to be. The ample culture of Father Varela teaches us, in such an early period of the previous century, that there are those in the Americas who can contribute a great deal, not only to the very juridical structure of the inter-American constitutional order, but also to make valuable contributions to the European Continent.

The first remark made by Father Varela is addressed to define the scope of sovereignty and its juridical structure in the Constitution. He went on to say: "If we pay attention to the origin of power exercised by monarchs upon their peoples, or of any corporation, we notice that either force made them become the owners of what justice had not given them, or else their authority does not emanate but from the voluntary resignation that individuals have performed of a part of their freedom, on behalf of themselves and their countrymen. Effectively, by their very nature, all persons have equal rights and freedoms, but once assembled in large societies and diversified by their interests and passions, they need a direction and, even more, an authority that will keep them within their mutual rights, without allowing society to dissolve, nor its members to hurt each other." These are the foundations of democratic society, of a constituted nation, juridically and politically, as a state, and of respect to the sovereign will of the people and to the rights of each of its citizens.

Then he goes on to add: "This authority could not be exercised by all individuals, but it was in all of them because it was in the society, considering that no person had been installed who had it. They were installed, consequently did not receive any more power than that voluntarily given by society itself, which never intended to be enslaved to its government, nor to renounce its rights, its advancement and its perfection."

He continues: "Every goodness comes to us from God, and justice, which is one of the main virtues, cannot have any other origin; he who violates it offends God and will vainly try to justify himself before men, in order to elude those penalties imposed by law, since he is not only obligated by temporary fear, but also by conscience or responsibility before God. Society, as a moral body, has its rights, that no one may attack without violating justice; there is a covenant between peoples and the supreme authority, the fulfillment of which is an act of the same virtue, and this is the sense in which the Apostle speaks, which is applicable to any kind of government, and not precisely to the monarchic kind, since the divine letters are not arranged by the institutions of men, but by the essential justice of God."

Father Varela underlines that: "We must, therefore, give Caesar what is his, which is something limited to a temporary authority granted by the people, and that no individual ought to disobey. Let us give God what is His, observing His Holy Law and essential duties of justice, in any form of society, but let it be never said that a just and merciful God has wished to deprive men of their rights, that He Himself gave them through their nature."

"The government exerts functions of sovereignty, it does not own them, nor can it claim to be their owner."

"One of the results of true liberty is the right to equality, that means: the right to have perfection's and merits appreciated in the same manner as any other equal ones found in any individual, so as that one action will not lose because of the person who executes it. There are three kinds of equality: The natural one, which consists of the identity of kind and nature, because all men have the same principles and, in general, the same things are convenient and repugnant to them. The social one, consisting of equal participation in the social wealth, due to the equal influx of all individuals, and the legal one, which is based upon the attribution of rights and imposition of prizes and penalties without any differentiation among persons. The natural and social kinds of equality are necessarily accompanied by an inequality, since men in nature, albeit consisting of the same principles and having the same rights of the species, are differentiated in the individual perfection's, be they bodily or intellectual... Legal equality is found in the distribution of rights, and is the only one not accompanied by inequality..."

Finally, Father Varela states, referring to LIBERTY and EQUALITY: "Peoples lose their freedom either by a tyrant's oppression or by the malice and ambition of some individuals, who avail themselves of the same people to enslave them, while they proclaim their sovereignty. The first method is well known and even the most ignorant fight against a tyrant's injustices; the second one is less perceptible and usually escapes even the more versed politicians. If the exercise of the sovereignty of the people has no limits, its representatives, who consider themselves as its owners, could become despots and, at times, the lowly interests of one party would shape the disgrace of the nation." Father Varela's prophetic vision, over one and a half century ago, has unfortunately been fulfilled in his own people.

The first professorship of International Law that he inaugurated in the Americas and projected in the juridical, normative and theological orders, as well as in the political and social orders, are presently the foundation for the rights of human beings and of peoples.

MAN, SOCIETY, STATE AND GOVERNMENT:
HISTORICAL SEQUENCE

We must follow a historical sequence in order to learn the evolution that has been experimented by the conception of man, the organization of societies, the State and the Government, and what their implications have been for the enforcement of the full dignity of man in his historical environment.

For this analysis, we must base ourselves upon the conception of man that was held since the most primitive social organization until our times, observing how, in that historical process, the present conjunction of man's problems has developed, leading us to arise the confrontation between ANTHROPOCENTRISM and THEOCENTRISM.

In the primitive societies, developed before the advent of Christianity, there prevailed an anthropocentric conception of the world, man and his relationships within society, apart from his origin and relationships. Everything developed around man, his necessities, what he thought about himself and everything which surrounded him, with a dimension limited by the scope of his rational vision, his capability for perceiving himself, and the primitive society or community to which he belonged. It was an anthropocentric cosmovision, polytheistic and pagan.

The degree of progress or civilization that man and his organization could attain, or what we could define as his degree of civilization, was outside of any transcendental dimension.

Although we can point out some variants in time and history, the civilizations that could be encompassed within this classification, essentially anthropocentric and polytheists, would be: The Egyptian, Greek and Roman ones and, in the Americas, the Aztec, Mayan and Incan, because those of the Siboney and Taino, such as others belonging to lesser nuclei in the Americas, do not have the importance of the former.

Man, imprisoned by an anthropocentric conception, would start from himself, advance up to where the initial momentum would take him, and develop in the material order up to where his purely human creative strength could reach, with no point of reference outside of his own environment and, once a certain level of development had been achieved, he would exhaust his impelling force, would retreat upon himself and start the process of weakening his own strength, because of the purely human limit initially set around man, that is, an anthropocentric one. They were thus gradually disappearing one after another, leaving some visible signals of their presence in history for us, but without these being able to serve as foundations to reach the levels that we have attained today, with reference to man himself and his human rights.

The historical cycle of that anthropocentric conception of man is broken with the appearance of the Hebrew people in history, which opens the door of communication with God, separating them from man. The Old Testament picks up that fundamental change in the history of humankind. That relationship of man and God, that theocentric dimension, essentially based upon REVELATION and the TEN COMMANDMENTS. We could find , in the Old Testament, that communication that Hebrews have with God.

What interests us about that substantial change of the theocentric cosmovision of man and his relationship with God, is the historical importance that it had in recognizing two fundamental things: (a) That man, in his anthropocentric cosmovision, was limited to himself, exhausted himself and the civilization or human organization based upon that conception of himself ended up by disappearing, because of the limitation in man's own capability; (b) That it contributed a new dimension which, because of it being focused towards the Infinite, did not exhaust itself, but had its own strength while conscience and belief in its God would be maintained.

The Greek people, later on, contributed a new philosophy based upon thought, in the successive acts of thinking, but in an intellectual, abstract context. They gave us the convenience of going from one idea to another, a useful dialect for this concatenation of ideas, albeit eminently theoretical. They set aside the conception of man in his dual dimension: Human and divine. With emphasis upon the purely intellectual task, they neglected the mechanics of man's material production, were very far from what man could achieve in his work of modification and production, in the necessary methods to attain a technology that would be useful for their development.

This historical cycle, that extended until the advent of Christianity, will allow us to perceive more clearly the elements that will help us to understand what we today call: THE DIGNITY OF THE HUMAN PERSON AND HIS/HER RIGHTS AND ATTRIBUTES.

The appearance of Christianity transformed man's cosmovision, his origin and his relationship. It established the unshakable foundations for the inalienable and imprescriptible rights of man, made in God's image and likeness and the possessor of divine and human attributes that are beyond the jurisdiction of men, who could no longer limit them, nor change, violate or surpress them without attempting, not only against man himself, but also against his conduct towards God. (The monotheism of other societies participates in this trend.)

Man's free will, absolute freedom to choose the road towards good or evil, would be a most important factor in the dynamics of History since then.

The appearance of Christianity starts what we call "Christian Civilization," that would powerfully contribute to better and uplift man, and consequently, those societies where he develops.

Christianity also incorporates, in a very valuable historical synthesis, the Hebrew idea of the relationship of man and God, and the Greek idea of reasoning. The contributions of Christianity and that synthesis, a product of its appearance in History, shape the new man brought about by those currents of thought and religiosity, and the concept of the rights of man begins to get attention, albeit initially they are not picked up by International Law nor in the existing legislation.

Hebrew and Christian thinkers advance on a path that has vertical lines towards God and horizontal lines towards man.

St. Augustine finds the theological elements that allow him to establish the parameters of the <u>historical conscience of man</u>, beginning with his relationship with God, in his work "The City of God."

The appearance of Christ in History, a fact that nobody can deny because it would tantamount to deny History, set new parameters in the conception of the world, the person and his/her own nature, as well as his/her innate rights (for Christians, God became man, God-Man.)

When man finds a point of reference beyond the scope of the vision of his intelligence, he will have since then an inexhaustible fountain and a dynamic one to impel his life towards God, producing along the way everything that could spring from his liberty, from his free will, from his private initiative, from his right to decide his own life with no interference's that would denaturalize its essence, albeit with the natural limitations that he, himself, will freely impose to live within society and keep the harmony, serving the common good.

Saint Thomas Aquinas effected a great contribution to this theocentric cosmovision of man, in his work entitled "Summa Theologica," that achieves an indisputable synthesis between Faith and Reason, but subordinates the latter to the former; thence we could derive, more than from any other source, modern technology and science. Thomism is a valuable contribution in that direction.

The human being is God's creature and, therefore in that condition must continue the work of CREATION, but within the parameters created by God, albeit with full freedom to choose, since God only limited Himself in that freedom that He gave men.

The enormous momentum that Christian civilization achieved in its beginnings, was due to the way in which these basic elements of the conception of man and the world operated, and the rights and freedoms of same as factors in the creation.

The respect, protection and guarantee of human rights and their exercise within the environment of the Christian society, gave the pre-Renaissance Christianity a dynamics that would be slowed later on.

The ancient Manicheism, the struggle between good and evil, once again appears after the pagan, pre-Christian civilizations had been overcome, which exhausted their potential around man in concentric circles, in their anthropocentric cosmovision.

Religious doctrines and ideologies were developed that, besides denying free will, by invoking God reestablished the basic principles of anthropocentrism, already overcome by Christianity.

A conceptual dichotomy is established regarding man, his essential equality, his origin as God's creature, free and the owner of his destiny, and in exchange we are told about chosen person and condemned persons, even before they are born, from there an erroneous conception of the State, the Government, power, society and sovereignty would derive.

The inequality established by those doctrines and ideologies was going to have an impact with a great historical transcendency in human relations, since there would be individuals who would be interned to serve and others would have the privilege of being served, which is a blatant violation of human rights. The distorting effects of that false conception about human beings, in their human and divine dimensions, are being endured by all nowadays.

German philosopher Emmanuel Kant, the author of "Critique of Pure Reason," a promoter of the historical-critical school in the 18th. century, believed that philosophical discussion must occur at the empirical and scientific levels, marginating the mysterious and divine, the transcendental sense.

At the end of the 18th. century, there appeared the ideas of German philosopher Hegel, who tried to restore the dialectical course of history that had been distorted and disarticulated by religious and ideological doctrines.

Hegel's dialectics teaches us that with a given historical situation, which he classified as "thesis," other situations are going to be found which deny the former; he called the latter "antithesis." From the collision and confrontation of both there will come a "synthesis," and so forth, without any permanent historical situation existing.

Hegel could not escape the ideas of his times; that is why he bases his ideas upon necessity and not upon liberty, whereby he makes a mistake that invalidates his thesis and is likely, as it happened in reality, to foster attempts to steal his ideas in order to support doctrines, ideologies or systems that violate the basic principles of the dignity of human beings, their freedoms and their rights.

It has been historically demonstrated that the basic motor of History is not necessity, but liberty. Those who have made the mistake of confounding both, have done great harm to humanity, of which we have no yet recovered, especially regarding the innate human rights of men and women and the development, progress and stability of our societies.

This ideological-philosophical foundation of Hegel's, strongly influenced by positivism, gave way to what Karl Marx called "dialectical materialism" and to the publication of his best known work: "Das Kapital."

Marx starts from two false premises: Hegel's dialectics, based upon necessity, and the capitalist society that he sees in Europe, especially in England, whose capitalistic society he deems as a static model as to the working people's well-being, and progressing towards a greater control of all means of production. He confounds society and state, and assigns the government a function that he stresses so that it will have room within his doctrine.

Marx advocates the nonexistence of God, which would imply the negation of the origin of human beings, since these, as God's creatures, has been created by Him, who for Marx does not exist, then whence do human beings come from? Where do all their rights come from? Out of that false conception about human beings, God and the world, there he issues his thesis about class struggle and the dictatorship of the proletariat, thus restoring the exploitation of the self-elected (the New-Class, in the words of Milovan Djilas) upon the reprobate, who would be all of those belonging to the group of the defeated (or their descendants) in the class struggle.

Through this, the worst of all servitude's: Exploitation of human beings by the state, would take place.

Although Marx did not intend to create a totalitarian state, he did set the basis for same. But it was Vladimir Ilytch Ulianov, a.k.a. Lenin, who identified the State-Government-Power, and created that monster of our times that is the totalitarian state, which upon creating its system assumes all the rights of the human person, that it does not deem as innate, inalienable, imprescriptible nor derived from others. They simply do not exist, cannot be pitted against the supreme authority of the Marxist-Leninist Totalitarian State. Here we have and INSTITUTIONAL VIOLATION OF HUMAN RIGHTS in its dual dimension: INSTITUTIONAL and HUMAN. Upon these violations coming about, the dignity of the human person is being denied, his/her freedom and all of their attributes. It totally ignores, and therefore denies, free will, private initiative and its dynamics, and transfers to the State the initiative and control of society, of the human person and his/her rights. The identity of the individual is suffocated, getting him/her to become a piece, an instrument of the totalitarian state, devoid of the will to do and lacking any of their own initiative; with no liberty to decide his/her destiny. Thus, human beings lost their futures under those regimes.

Human beings, in this absorbing and totalitarian system, have conscience of their helplessness; they know that they are unarmed vis-à-vis the totalitarian power and they direct their energies and their wills towards the basic necessities, longing the loss of their freedom and of their condition of persons in their dual dimension: Human and of divine origin. This has come to be in the Soviet Union, the satellite nations and also in Cuba.

When Christ resurrected, who is God and Man for Christians, He placed Himself outside of history, and became the goal, the universal reference for human beings.

From this starting point, human beings will follow that path, correcting it in accordance with the message, and in possession of all the attributes that are required to attain the most high of aspirations, while, participating in the creation, they continue their upward path, rectifying mistakes and correcting their course, while at the same time working and producing for themselves, for their offspring, for the society to which they belong and for the advancement of technology within the Christian Mystic-dialectics, that will serve them as an instrument, as a compass in the upward path of life.

Christian civilization has been infiltrated by the influence of religious and ideological doctrines that are in crisis today, and which have hampered the upward process of humankind, taking science away from humanities and giving things scientific a preeminence while limiting the spiritual and moral development of human beings.

Those countries that have not followed the religious doctrinarian orientation, getting away from the concept of God-Man and deforming and shackling the freedoms of the human person, have descended not only in their levels of family living, their regional and societal living, but also in their relationships with other nations.

Anthropocentric cosmovision, running counter to theocentric cosmovision, has erupted anew, also running counter to the idea of God in history and outside of it. This is retrogression.

This regressive transculturation has stagnated the spiritual, moral and material development of humankind and has brought about unthinkable degradation's, such as those that produced the Holocaust against Jews, the interpretation of which has to be sought not only inside of the narrow limits of a race, but in what it meant for the substitution of paganism and the incorporation of its God as a mandatory reference point in its life and its actions in History.

Since for Karl Marx "religion is the opium of the peoples," a product of the capitalistic superstructure, he obliterates all references to God and confuses the dynamics of History; by starting from economics, he goes to the class struggle until "the new class" will have swept away the former one, but without any transcendental objective and also incapacitating that "new class," immersed in doctrine, for the realization of the human being, who once he/she has destroyed what they found, is incapable of creating, because that latter was not included in their theoretical budget.

The kind of materialistic collectivism generated by that doctrine also exhausts itself, unable to leave, with the ideal or doctrinarian instruments that it owns, from the cyclical process that leads it to its own annihilation. Hence its attempts for openings towards Christian civilizations, in the technological, economical, commercial fields, and in some minor concessions of freedom for the human person.

Every time that small measure of freedom has been given to human beings, the ruling class has been astonished and full of fears, because of the surprising success that human beings have attained, and which, through that process, threaten the survival of the self-elected. That is why, as soon as they can do it, they again surpress freedom, until the system will again need a small safety valve for the pressures that human beings, consciously or not, exert upon the all-embracing power of the totalitarian state.

The Marxist-Leninist system enshrines in its constitutions and the whole of its legislation the instruments and institutions that supplant the values and principles of the Western Judeo-Christian civilization, establishing in lieu of the former those others that replace them with enough clarity so that nobody will be confused as to which their true objectives are: To replace a system by another, the latter being inefficient and inept.

In a nation as close as Cuba is, we can observe with a high degree of clarity the mechanisms that are used by Marxism-Leninism to replace s system with another. That is the only country in the Americas in which that political phenomenon has taken place, which threatens not only all nations in this Hemisphere, but also the world as a whole.

It is not in this book where we will demonstrate the application of strategies and tactics leading to that replacement of a system by another; we will only refer to the implications that said replacement had with regard to the dignity of the human person, his/her freedom and all of their inalienable, innate and imprescriptible attributes, and the violations of same in their two dimensions: INSTITUTIONAL and HUMAN.

THE U.S. CONSTITUTION AND HUMAN RIGHTS

It is pertinent that we say, when referring to the theme of human rights, the relationship that exists for their protection between the rulers and the governed.

As we have seen, constitutional law is present in the beginning, the development and the recognition of human rights and all freedoms they encompass. The Constitution, which as the fundamental law of the nation, organized as a State, is the guarantee in the national environment of the exercise and enjoyment of fundamental human rights. This has been historically verified since the Declaration of Independence of the United States, whose basic principles were incorporated in the Constitution of the United States in 1787. Then came the French Revolution and the same principles were incorporated to the Constitution of France in 1789.

Since then, the progressive process of Constitutional Law has been constant until our times.

The Constitution of the United States of America, since it was approved, has inspired most of the constitutions of the world. Out of the 172 countries in the world, over three fourths of them, that is, 160, have been inspired by the U.S. Constitution.

Four basic principles in the U.S. Constitution have been, one way or another, standard models for those constitutions. These are:

A. Human rights issued from the Creator, God.

B. Basic human rights are: Life, liberty and the pursuit of happiness.

C. Human rights are inalienable and imprescriptible, issued from a higher authority, upon whom neither human beings nor governments have any jurisdiction.

D. Sovereignty is inherent to the people; rulers are elected by the people in order to guarantee and respect human rights, not to violate them.

Many leaders of the Third World have publicly acknowledged the influence that the U.S. Constitution has had in their own constitutions.

India's former Prime Minister, Jawaharlal Nehru, stated before the U.S. Congress in 1949: "Our country and our constitution have been strongly influenced by the U.S. Constitution."

The ideologies that have projected their influences, over more than half of the 19th. century and a great deal of the 20th., have darkened and distorted that influence, which is regaining its importance upon the twilight of those ideologies, as we will see when dealing with this issue in regard to human rights.

This trend in constitutional standards comes about starting with the Bolshevik Revolution of 1917 and was extended to Germany under Hitler, to Italy under Mussolini and those nations subjugated by the Soviet Union, Cuba among them.

This differentiation is not whimsical or casuistic; it is one of the basic problems of our times. There is a distinct difference between those states that respect the human rights of their subjects and those others which violate or deny them; those which have institutionalized the violations of human rights and those who consecrate and respect human rights, as the case was with the Cuban Constitution of 1940.

Violations of human rights can be inherent to a system and inseparable from that system.

In a territory where a regime of law does not exist, a State of Law, there cannot be any respect nor guarantee for human rights. A free person must live, and he/she can only do so, in a state where freedom is respected, that is, in a free state.

When the state, in the exercise of the public power, assumes the rights of human beings with no limitation vis-à-vis its subjects, an institutional violation has take place; it is institutionalized, regardless of whatever pretext that may be invoked for the violation of human rights.

In this case, the violation is not the consequence but the cause from which the totalitarian state derives its power, other than from the free consent of its subjects. This is a substantial difference, that Marxists and crypto-Marxists have not yet fully understood; that is why they are confused and they attempt to confuse everyone else.

Marxists and their "traveling companions" sustain that Marxism, as an economic interpretation of History, does not have anything to do with the institutional violation of human rights, nor with the dignity of the human person. That fallacy has run a long way, and we want to contribute to its clarification, in order to prevent the world from continuing to be confused by it.

Karl Marx affirms, in an exaggeration to which these generalizing theoreticians are favorable, that it is the economy which determines the structure of peoples and development of History, that which generates the evolutionary process of humankind. He emphasizes that both men and women are born good and that the unjust economic structures make them bad; that is why, according to him, upon changing those structures, the human person will be changed.

There is a fundamental contradiction between that Marxist affirmation about birth, and Christianity's affirmation. For the latter, children are born with the original sin and this is erased by baptism, which makes them participants of the divinity, of the Mystical Body of Christ. Marxism's economic theories sweep aside all of that.

For Marxism, the human person will be good or bad depending upon the economic structures in which he/she lives, and they will be good when they change according to the guidelines issued by Marxism. This is another Marxist-Communist fallacy, that denies the dignity of the human person.

As it has proclaimed and practiced, Marxism, in order to put an end to the exploitation of human beings by other human beings, transfers to the State all of the human person's rights; it says that this is temporary, because it deems itself "the dictatorship of the proletariat, to finish all other social classes". What Marxism does, theoretically and practically, is changing from the theocentric cosmovision to the anthropocentric cosmovision.

These are other characteristics of Marxism:

    a.   It affirms that the economy determines and conditions History and culture. Everything issues from the economy, and it attributes to the economy, the surging of religions and superstitions, which it deems as "the opium of the peoples", as Karl Marx said.

b.   It stifles private initiative, transferring to the State, the control of the economy, with the ill-fated results that we already know.

c.   Establishes a totalitarian dictatorship (deceivingly called "the dictatorship of the proletariat"), which suffocates all human rights at both levels: INSTITUTIONAL and HUMAN.

d.   Creates a monstrous state capitalism, inefficient and inept.

e.   It absorbs surplus value, in order to nurture with it a hypertrophied and inept bureaucracy, that it needs to keep their subjects in a condition of submission.

f.   It violates freedom, free will and self-determination of the individual, who is forced to follow the guidelines issued by the State, which controls everything. The economy will be directed by "the new class" and that leads it to it's its inefficiency and ultimate destruction.

Dogmatic Marxists, as any other ideological dogmatists, continue to be adhered to their Marxist theory, saying that what has been implemented in all Marxist-subjugated countries that there have been, is not Marxism proper, but a deformation of the same. Thus, not even the irrefutable evidence offered today by Communist or Marxist regimes all over the world would be enough to destroy their hallucination, because of a simple reason: This kind of hallucinations and theories are not destroyed, neither by evidence nor by reality.

The conclusion that we must reach is that the economic interpretation of History by Karl Marx is false, and that when it kills private initiative, the innate kindness of the human beings, and makes his/her spiritual and material development fall upon economic structures, it is violating the dignity of the human person, his/her freedom, free will and self-determination.

Thus, affirming that the Marxist economic interpretation of History has nothing to do with freedom, self-determination or the dignity of the human person, is tantamount to being ignorant about Marxism.

INTERNATIONAL LAW AND HUMAN RIGHTS

When we refer to the international norms for human rights, we must consider the difference between the Old International Law and the modern trends of International Law.

The Old School of International Law left at the mercy of states and their internal legislation the guarantee and the respect for human rights. It did not consider the individual, the human person, as a subject of law, because of which it was deemed as incapable of affording any protection to human rights, since its jurisdiction did not reach the human person as such.

After World War II, the Jewish Holocaust and other monstrosities committed against the person, the world hastened to give the human person the condition of <u>subject of the law.</u> First in a subjective order, in the theoretical awarding of certain rights, until then forbidden to the individual, and later on in a more concrete manner, as a subject of the law, but without this declarative evolution of rights being able to have a territorial scope for its application, nor a coercive authority for its enforcement.

In the human rights declarations of the United States of America, in its Constitution and in its Bill of Rights, in the British influence towards the people, as a collective vis-à-vis- the sovereign, in the French Revolution that incorporates the U.S. Bill of Rights; at the end of World War II and, in part, as a consequence of same, the AMERICAN DECLARATION OF THE RIGHTS AND DUTIES OF MAN is written on April, 1948; the UNIVERSAL DECLARATION OF HUMAN RIGHTS of the United Nations, approved on December 10, 1948, and Helsinki Accords, in 1975.

In order to ascertain the progressive trend that shapes modern International Law and the Declarations and Covenants of Human Rights brought about after these declarations, we must go to the analysis of the behavior of this trend for human rights at the international level.

Both in the International Law and in the Declarations of Human Rights, as well as in the covenants, the fundamental issue is the human person, his/her dignity, his/her freedom and all of his/her attributes. We must go back to the human person in his/her dual dimension: Horizontal towards everything that surrounds him/her, relatives, community, nation, state, and vertical towards God.

The evolution of International Law is directed to consider the human person as a subject of the law, basically to guarantee and protect his/her human rights above all boundaries and beyond the jurisdictional reach of each State. All of that must be performed while seeking to attain ideal goals of respect for those rights and favorable environments for their exercise.

The leader of the United States of America, Franklin Delano Roosevelt, and of Great Britain, Winston Churchill, proclaimed on August, 1941, the four freedoms that they deemed basic, emphasizing the freedom from fear. Those four freedoms referred to the conduct of the human person, his/her manifestations and the respect that the States had to observe towards them, as well as the guarantees that had to be provided. These are: Freedom of expression, freedom of religion, the right to be protected as to material needs, and freedom from fear.

These freedoms served as complements for the basic human rights, such as life and liberty, and were included in the human rights declarations of the Americas and of the United Nations upon the end of World War II.

That war, with its tragic consequences, still served to impel the normative process for the protection of human rights.

The Atlantic Charter, as that proclamation of human rights was called, was received with shows of gladness in the world, and gave way to the birth of great expectations in order to hasten a new universal structure that would afford a greater protection to the human person in his/her inalienable and imprescriptible rights.

The universal movement on behalf of human rights would be reflected, first in declarations and later on in conventions, which have structured norms and guarantee measures for human rights.

Among them, we have the following:

a. The American Declaration of the Rights and Duties of Man, the first to be proclaimed, on April 1948, in Bogota, Colombia.
b. The Universal Declaration of Human Rights, on December 10, 1948.
c. The European Convention for Protection of Human Rights and Fundamental Liberties, 1950.
d. International Covenants about Human Rights, in 1967.

e.   American Convention o Human Rights, 1967.

f.   Helsinki Accords, 1975.

These declarations and conventions, together with the Atlantic Charter and the historical background that we have mentioned, would be the basic elements of that process for the protection and guarantee of the exercise of human rights.

With regard to the American Declaration of the Rights and Duties of Man, we must feature interesting aspects.

First: It is the only Declaration of Human Rights that indicates duties at the same time.

Second: That the international communist movement (Komintern) tried to prevent the juridical and political structuration of the Organization of American States (O.A.S.) in Bogota, Colombia.

Third: That the Komintern tried to prevent the approval of the American Declaration of the Rights and Duties of Man in Bogota, Since such a declaration runs totally counter to the Marxist-Leninist doctrine, which does not recognize these rights for the human person, but instead dispossesses him/her of said rights and transfers them to the totalitarian State, to the Dictatorship of the Proletariat, in the face of which the human person remains helpless, undefended.

They were willing to pay any price to prevent those events from taking place in Bogota, and they would use all available means in this Hemisphere to attain their goal.

The expansionist strategy of Marxism-Leninism brought about a historical event known as the "Bogotazo" (the Bogota revolt) in which activists of the Communist Party of Colombia and other countries participated, among them, Fidel Castro Ruz, whose activities there have been verified.

The "Bogotazo" resulted in over five thousand deaths and great damages for the capital of Colombia, and endangered the continuation of the NINTH INTER-AMERICAN CONFERENCE. Only the solid determination of the American States and the attitude of the Colombian Government were able to overcome all obstacles in order to go ahead with the Conference and attain such important agreements, that changed the juridical and political face of the Americas and provided the nations of this Hemisphere with instruments that would allow them to counter the extra-continental intervention of international communism in the Americas.

We must underline that the Americas were getting ready to afford protection to Human rights and guarantee the exercise of same, which is capital threat for the Marxist-Leninist doctrine. The elements committed to the world communist movement mobilized and attacked. We must ask ourselves: "Why?" In the answer that we give to that question we shall find that, while the Western World did not consider that it was attacking the foundations of the international communist movement, the latter did believe that and tried to hamper everything that could mean an obstacle in its path for the expansion of its doctrine.

We have to add, upon referring to the American Convention on Human Rights and the Creation of the Inter-American Court of Human Rights, signed in Costa Rica, that here is an ADDITIONAL PROTOCOL TO THE AMERICAN CONVENTION ON HUMAN RIGHTS, that comes to consolidate the guarantees established in the Convention and its enhancement towards the democratic institutions, personal freedom, social justice and the economic and cultural rights.

In its preamble, said Protocol underlines the following:

"The States which are Parties to this Additional Protocol to the American convention on Human Rights,

"In reaffirming their purpose of consolidating in this Continent, within the framework of democratic institutions, a regime of personal freedom and social justice, based upon the respect for the essential rights of man,

"In recognizing that the essential rights of man are not born of the fact of his/her being a national of a certain State, but that they have as their foundation the attributes of the human person, for which reason they merit an international protection, of a conventional nature, be it cooperating or complementary, to that which is offered by the internal law of the American States,

"Considering the close relationship existing between the enforcement and economic, social and cultural rights, and that of civil and political rights, since both categories of rights make an indissoluble whole that finds its foundation in the recognition of the dignity of the human person, because of which both demand a permanent protection and promotion with the purpose of

40

attaining their full enforcement, <u>without the possibility of ever justifying the violation of some of them for the sake of the realization of others"</u>.

In this last paragraph, the additional protocol to the Convention is touching the most sensitive spot of the Marxist-Leninist propaganda, the latter affirming that some rights must be sacrificed for the sake of others, with which the human person is left without any of those rights, as it has happened in all countries where such a doctrine has been implemented; in the Americas, we have the example in Cuba.

This is not a conventional movement isolated from the Americas on behalf of the human person, but it is also the preoccupation of other regions and institutions that promote respect for the human person.

It is timely to quote here the last Encyclical from Pope John Paul II, entitled (in Latin) "SOLLICITUDO REI SOCIALIS" (On Social Concerns) in which he reaffirms that the vital issue in our time is <u>respect for the dignity of the human person</u>, that must be defended and protected vis-à-vis whoever tries to diminish his/her rights, guarantees and possibilities.

The Pontifical zeal tries to surround the human person with all of the guarantees and safeguards for the full development of his/her dignity and of all of their human rights.

Progress has been made in the process of protecting human rights, not only in declarations, but also in various conventions and others juridical instruments. Let us examine some of these:

1.   The Geneva Convention about War Prisoners.

2.   The Convention of La Habana, Cuba, on the Right to Asylum (1928).

3.   The Convention for the Prevention and Sanction of the Crime of Genocide (1948).

4.   Convention on the Stature for Refugees (1951).

5.   Convention on Political Rights for Women (1952).

6.   Convention on Slavery (Modification Protocol - 1953).

7.   Convention on the Statute for Stateless Persons (1954).

8.   Complementary Convention on the Abolition of Slavery (1956).

9.   Convention on the Nationality of Married Women (1957).

10.   Convention to Reduce the Cases of Stateless Persons (1961).

11.   Convention on Consent for Marriage, the Minimum Age to Marry and Registry of Marriages (1962).

12.   Convention on all Forms of Racial Discrimination (1965).

13.   International Convention on Labor (1921).

14.   International Red Cross Convention.

15.   United Nations Convention on Torture.

16.   Convention on Torture of the Organization of American States (O.A.S.).

Both declarations and covenants and treaties clash against juridical obstacles, some times insurmountable, for their application to those states that provide in their constitutions or jurisprudence that no treaty or convention may interfere or diminish the contents of said constitutions. The prevalence of internal law vis-à-vis international law is an issue that advances slowly, but it progresses. We must point out that the greatest advancement attained as to international law has been regarding human rights, especially in the Americas, the cradle of declarative birth and of constitutional protection for these rights.

ABOUT THE INTER-AMERICAN COMMISSION ON HUMAN RIGHTS

The Fifth Meeting of Consultation of External Relations Ministers, assembled in the Republic of Chile on August, 1959, approved Resolution No. VIII, whereby the Inter-American Commission on Human Rights of the Organization of American States (OAS) was created.

The Statutes that would rule this Commission until 1965 were approved on May 25, 1960, which powers were enhanced by the Extraordinary Inter-American Conference.

In the Second Extraordinary Inter-American Conference, the Commission's authorizations were enlarged, in order for same to be enabled not only to exercise promotion activities, but also the protection of human rights.

A great step forward had been taken towards international regulation upon granting the human person the right to denounce the violation of human rights before international organisms. Up to that date, only the States could formulate denouncements about violations of the human rights of their subjects or of the States as such. Now, individuals could do that on their own right, against their own States or against other States. International Law has been enriched in a remarkable manner.

In that second Extraordinary Inter-American Conference, at Rio de Janeiro, two resolutions were approved, among others: The XXII and the XXIV, which tended to strengthen the jurisdictional scope of the Commission and of its powers. The XXII enhances the powers of the Inter-American Commission on Human Rights, and entrusts it with the continuation of its watch for the enforcement and faithful observance of human rights in all member States of the OAS, and urges it to take into account, especially, the observance of human rights encompassed in Articles I, II, III, IV, XVIII, XXV and XXVI of the American Declaration of the Rights and Duties of Man.

The Draft to Reform the OAS Charter, prepared in Panamá, would deal with the Commission in two of its chapters, the XVIII and XXV.

These two chapters were approved in the III Extraordinary Inter-American Conference, held in 1967, and were incorporated into the Buenos Aires Protocol as Articles 112 and 150. The Commission was granted conventional juridical status and its authority was strengthened as the organism for human rights.

The two articles listed above had a final phrasing as follows:

Article 112.   There shall be an Inter-American Commission on Human Rights, which shall have as its primary function that of promoting the observance and defense of human rights, and serving as advisory organ for the Organization (of American States) in this matter.

An Inter-American Convention on Human Rights shall determine the structure, competence and procedures of said Commission, as well as those of the other organs in charge of this matter.

Article 150.   While the Inter-American Commission on Human Rights referred to in Chapter XVIII is not in force, the present Inter-American Commission on Human Rights shall be entrusted with the observance of said rights.

The Inter-American Commission on Human Rights (IACHR) has received, in the intervening conferences and assemblies of the OAS, a greater juridical backing, not only to promote, but also to guard and protect human rights in the Hemisphere, among the member States of the OAS.

It received denouncements from individual persons, contributing to the strengthening and enhancement of the International Public Law in the Americas; it effected in-situ investigations; it granted hearings for individuals and collectivities from the member States. It prepared special reports on the condition of human rights in several member States. Every year, it submits an annual report to the Ordinary General Assembly of the OAS.   In special cases, it approves resolutions.

The IACHR has been limited by those countries that do not allow investigations on their territories (in loco), as in the case of Cuba; also, because of the duty it has to await the exhaustion of the internal channels. In many cases, that way of the international channels takes forever, because of the deficiencies in its procedural system, of alien or external political influences, of fears to bring about a crisis in the state and, finally, for lack of international resources.

THE INTER-AMERICAN COMMISSION ON HUMAN RIGHTS AND CUBA

The Inter-American Commission on Human Rights of the OAS was created in 1959 precisely because of Cuba having fallen under a communist regime, whose Marxist-Leninist doctrine is incompatible with the principles, values and rights that said Commission is obligated to guard, promote and protect.

The Commission is made up by all member states of the OAS, which submit to the Ordinary General Assembly of the OAS, its maximum organism, nominations of candidates in order to elect seven members, who despite coming from the states that nominated them, shall act within the Commission, not on behalf of their respective countries, but on a personal capacity.

The first denouncement about violations of human rights was received in 1961 on Cuba, "submitted by Drs. Guillermo Martinez Marquez and Claudio F. Benedi", as it has been documented by the illustrious Chilean jurist, Dr. Manuel Bianchi, who was its second chairman.

We have since submitted, in a continuous and uninterrupted manner, denouncements on the violations of human rights in Cuba, and we have contributed to document seven reports about violations of human rights in Cuba, in which our doctrine has been incorporated about INSTITUTIONAL AND HUMAN VIOLATIONS OF HUMAN RIGHTS.

Distinguished jurists from Latin-America, the United States of America and the Caribbean have been members of the Board of Directors of the Commission.

Since the beginning of its work, the Commission has requested to be allowed to investigate "in loco" on Cuban territory, and the communist regime has denied it that permission; it has finally refused to answer the requests and solicitations from the IACHR.

In accordance with the legal precepts that rule the Commission, governments which are accused before it for alleged violations of human rights on their respective territories, are granted a sufficiently extensive period of time to answer the denunciations or to reject them; should they elect not to do that, after said period having elapsed, the Commission shall deem that the denounced deeds have been proven. The denouncements are, in turn, investigated by the Commission by other means, with contributions and information that allow it to make a definitive judgment about the guilt of the infractor government, and to issue a ruling through the approval of the resolution, the special report or the annual report, as the case may be.

Should this procedure not be followed, violations of human rights would remain unpunished through such a simple procedure as it would be if the accused government did not acknowledge receipt of the requests made by the Commission. This is the assimilation of the juridical principle applied to a person convicted "in absentia", with the difference that, in this case, a procedural processing has been performed towards the accused, which is of a paramount importance: The transfer of the denouncement and the granting of a time period to answer it, timely and in due form.

Some members of the Inter-American Community have tried to help the Cuban regime with its constant violations of human rights, in attempting to take it out of the Commission's jurisdiction upon saying that "Cuba is not a member of the OAS and, therefore, its legal norms cannot be applied to Cuba." This thesis lacks totally any juridical value and, every time it has been submitted, we have defeated it one way or another. The juridical basis for that defeat is very simple: "What is outside of the Inter-American System and of the OAS is the present government of Cuba, because of its being Marxist-Leninist; but the Cuban State continues to be a member of the OAS."

In the Eighth Consultative Meeting of Foreign Relations Ministers, assembled in accordance with the Reciprocal Assistance Treaty, better known as the "Treaty of Rio," which sessions were held at Punta del Este, Uruguay, in 1962, it was agreed to declare that the Marxist-Leninist doctrine is "incompatible with the Inter-American System." It was agreed that if any government identified itself with the Marxist-Leninist doctrine, the same would be left out of the System and that, because the present government of Cuba had identified itself with the Marxist-Leninist doctrine, it was outside of the System.

It was in this opportunity, in 1962, in the Eighth Consultative Meeting, when the present government of Cuba was left out of the System and of the OAS, and not in the Ninth Consultative Meeting of Foreign Affairs Ministers, held in July, 1964; in the latter, the Marxist-Leninist regime of Cuba was sanctioned because of intervening in the internal affairs of Venezuela and of its being an aggressor, after verifying the denunciation from the

President of Venezuela, Don Rómulo Betancourt, a leader of democracy in the Americas.

The agreements of the Eighth Consultative Meeting of Foreign Relations Ministers, held in Uruguay in 1962, set a landmark in the political history of the Americas and a reaffirmation of the values and principles that shape the Inter-American System, as an expounder of Western Civilization and a supporter of same.

Two fundamental events are featured from that most important and historical meeting, i.e.:

1.   The Marxist-Leninist doctrine was declared incompatible with the Inter-American System.

        Whoever shall not participate in its principles and values, born of the Western Judeo-Christian Civilization and its Theocentrical cosmovision, is sanctioned with exclusion from the System.

2.   A new international law principle is established: The separation, regarding a multinational organization such as the OAS, between government and State. The government may be usurped and the State may be seized. But the seizing of the State does not denaturalize the State, nor makes it to lose its condition as such; however, the usurpation of the government would have negative effects; for those reasons, the Inter-American System does not tolerate within its organizations a foreign body that harms and affects it, which in this case is the government.   But the Cuban State continues to be a member of the OAS, which is an entity made up by States and not by governments.

But the most transcendental event that took place in this Eighth Consultative Meeting was the most important political statement in the history of the Inter-American System, consisting of the reaffirmation of the values and principles that shape it: The dignity of the human person, his/her freedom and attributes, the right of sovereignty, the participation of the people in the election of its rulers. Otherwise, democratic rights would not only be temporally limited or hampered, but totally suppressed.

With this Declaration of Punta del Este, the first confrontation in the Americas took place between two antagonist systems that fought for the world hegemony: Western Judeo-Christian Civilization, which is Theocentrical, reaffirming its belief in God and underlining that human beings have been created by God and given attributes and values that reaffirm their dignity and which are innate, inalienable and imprescriptible, which are conventionally called HUMAN RIGHTS, vis-à-vis the system that denies the existence of God. If God does not exist, where do human beings come from? It therefore denies the divine issue of human beings, their vertical relationship with God. These are two totally antagonist systems, irreconcilable, that encompass human beings in their entirety, both the peoples and the world.

The Inter-American System has, once again, attained the feat of sending a message with an utmost importance to the peoples of Europe and of the rest of the world, pointing out the path they must follow in this struggle, in which "not even the stars can be natural."

Because of all of the above, the Inter-American Commission on Human Rights has stated having, and in reality it has, jurisdiction to learn about the violations of human rights in Cuba, as we have juridically continued to demonstrate. That is why, also, the Commission must and ought to apply in Cuba the sanctions and condemnation that pertain to the institutional and human violations of human rights.

In the book published by the Commission, entitled "TEN YEARS OF ACTIVITIES: 1971-1981", on page 322, it has emphasized that the achievement of the enforcement of economic, social and cultural rights "cannot, in any case, justify the violations of fundamental political and civil rights..." This is a response to the supporters of the other system, who falsely say that "the economic interpretation of history is that it determines the conduct of human beings and of the peoples" and that all the other "alleged" rights must be sacrificed to it, such as the above mentioned human rights. The Inter-American System has risen to counter that first, and then the Inter-American Commission on Human Rights.

SEVEN REPORTS FROM THE INTER-AMERICAN COMMISSION ON HUMAN RIGHTS

The Inter-American Commission on Human Rights has approved and published seven reports. These are in chronological order:

A.   Report on the Status of Human Rights in Cuba (May 1, 1962).

B.   Report on the Status of Political Prisoners and Their Relatives in Cuba (May 17, 1963).

C.   Report on the Status of Human Rights in Cuba (April 27, 1967).

D.   Second Report on the Status of Political Prisoners and Their Relatives in Cuba (May 7, 1970).

E.   Fifth Report from the Inter-American Commission on Human Rights on the Status of Human Rights in Cuba (June 1, 1976).

F.   Sixth Report from the IACHR on the Status of Political Prisoners in Cuba (December 14, 1979).

G.   Seventh Report from the IACHR on the Status of Human Rights in Cuba (October 4, 1983).

The commission has approved the preparation of the eighth report which is now in the process of elaboration.

Amnesty International, from London, has been an important factor in the defense of human rights and the denouncement of their violations, including those in Cuba.

INSTITUTIONAL VIOLATION OF HUMAN RIGHTS IN CUBA, IN ITS DUAL DIMENSION: IN THE CONSTITUTION AND THE LAWS, AND IN THE HUMAN DIMENSION

We have denounced, since the beginning of the Marxist-Leninist regime in Cuba, those violations of human rights in their dual dimension, since the Inter-American Commission on Human Rights of the OAS started its work of guarding and protecting human rights. The institutional violation is in the Constitution and all laws that are in force in Cuba.

We denounce the nonexistence of a regime of law, of a State of law.

The Inter-American Commission on Human Rights (IACHR), in picking up our denouncements, has repeatedly condemned the nonexistence of a regime of law, of a State of law in Cuba.

Let us point out the latest denunciations that it has done against that situation. The Commission condemned it in its annual report to the Ordinary General Assembly of the OAS, held in Guatemala on November, 1986. In that report, among other things, it stated that in Cuba, "there are maintained, therefore, the two fundamental features that have given rise to the lack of enforcement of civil and political rights: The nonexistence of a state of law, since persons are deprived of those resources that would protect them from the actions of the State, and the lack of political alternatives for the populations." The Commission has kept itself within that framework of denouncements in its annual reports for 1987, 1988, 1989, 1990 and 1991.

The International Commission of Jurists, an organization ascribed to the United Nations Organization, performed an exhaustive study and investigation of the Cuban situation and concluded in its statement: "THE RULE OF LAW DOES NOT EXIST IN CUBA." That situation of nonexistence of the rule of law has been constantly maintained up to this date.

There does not exist, in Cuba, the division of powers which is fundamental in the juridical and political structure of modern states, in accordance with Montesquieu's definition.

The Judiciary Power is submitted to the so-called National Assembly of Popular Power, the same organism in charge of "approving" the pragmatism's dictated by the hierarchy of the Communist Party, which is the true power behind the throne. And the latter, in turn, is directed in a dictatorial fashion by the "maximum leader" on duty. All of this is stipulated in the Cuban Socialist Constitution of 1992, Articles 70, 85, 86, 87 et sequitur.

It would suffice to mention Article 62 of the Constitution above referred to, in order to conclude, without any shadow of doubt, that all human rights enshrined in the Western Civilization are violated in Cuba. Said article literally reads:

> "NONE OF THE FREEDOMS RECOGNIZED FOR CITIZENS CAN BE EXERCISED AGAINST THE DISPOSITIONS OF THE CONSTITUTION AND THE LAWS, NOR AGAINST THE EXISTENCE AND THE PURPOSES OF THE SOCIALIST STATE, NOR AGAINST THE DECISION BY THE CUBAN PEOPLE TO BUILD SOCIALISM AND COMMUNISM. THE VIOLATION OF THIS PRINCIPLE IS PUNISHABLE."

All human rights are violated by this statement; they are subjected to the "SOCIALIST STATE" and to the whims of the tyrant at hand who, on behalf of the construction of socialism and communism is empowered, by the Constitution and the laws, to violate with impunity all human rights. Thus, a juridical monstrosity would happen in Cuba: That it would be "legal" there to violate those human rights consecrated by God and recognized by our Western Civilization.

With this distressing perspective for the enforcement of human rights, it would perhaps be obvious that we began to analyze how each of those human rights consecrated by God is violated, which are recognized in the American Declaration of the Rights and Duties of Man and in the Declaration of Human Rights of the United Nations, not counting the Declaration of the European Community and its Parliament, and other multinational statements about human rights, but we believe it is convenient to do that, albeit only for a greater clarification of the objectives of this book.

In this century, when the Cuban people attained its independence, it gave itself freely a Constitution in 1901, in which there appeared the name of God in its preamble. Said invocation was a full ratification of the Cuban people's religious faith.

In 1940 again, the Cuban people, after a lengthy process, approved a new Constitution, in whose preamble the name of God was also written.

The present Marxist-Leninist regime in Cuba promulgated a socialist Constitution, published on the Official Gazette for Tuesday, February 24, 1976, in which it eliminated the name of God, thus ratifying at this time what it had already done in 1959, when it seized power by force. Thus was configured the basic objective of the new regime: The total elimination of the sense of transcendence, the elimination of the belief in God, the negation of God, which is intrinsic to any Marxist-Leninist regime, atheist and materialist, without adherence to the Christian morality nor to the moral principles that prevail in the Western World. They made the same elimination of God in the last Socialist Constitution of August 1, 1992.

AMERICAN DECLARATION OF THE RIGHTS AND DUTIES OF MAN

In its preamble it reads:

"All men are born free and equal in dignity and rights and, endowed as they are by nature with reason and conscience, must behave fraternally towards each other."

"The fulfillment of every one's duty is a requirement for the rights of others. Rights and duties correlatively integrate in every social and political activity of man. If rights extol individual freedom, duties express the dignity of that freedom."

"Duties of a juridical nature presuppose others of a moral nature, which conceptually support and establish them."

"It is man's duty to serve the spirit with all of his/her powers and resources, because the spirit is the supreme finality of human existence and its highest category."

"It is man's duty to exert, maintain and stimulate culture by all means at his/her disposal, because culture is the supreme social and historical expression of the spirit."

"And since morals and good manners are the noblest flowering of culture, it is every man's duty to respect them always."

Under the auspices of these principles and values, the sense of transcendence with the exaltation of the spirit, morals and culture, the Americas project in the Inter-American environment, in the Western Civilization of which it is a part, those inalienable and imprescriptible rights of men and women, prior to any rational or human regulation that may limit them, hamper or deform them and, of course, everything that will tend to violate or suppress them.

With this premise, let us go on to enumeration of those human rights enshrined in the American Declaration of Rights and Duties of Man, and in the Universal Declaration of Human Rights. We will analyze them in that order, in the chronological order in which they were approved, on April and December, 1948, forty six years ago.

[1]A.D. "Article 1. Every human being is entitled to life, freedom and the integrity of his/her person."

[2]U.D. "Article 1. All human beings are born free and equal in dignity and rights, and endowed as they are with reason and conscience, must behave fraternally towards each other."

We must analyze separately each of the fundamental rights of the Cuban people, in order to better understand the scope of the violations against them.

The violation of the fundamental right to life, which is the first and foremost in men and women, since all others issue from it. Let us repeat what Alphonse X, the Wise, said: "whoever deprives me of life, is depriving me of all of my other rights."

As to the present regime in Cuba, we can divide the violation of the right to life in two groups: First, the deprivation of life at the "execution wall" without any previous trial, or through a mockery passing as a trial, without any of the most elementary procedural guarantees, sentences imposed by kangaroo courts made up by fanatics and/or legal illiterates, sentences pre-dictated by the regime's leaders, including those who have lost their lives even without those "formalities"; and second, those deaths occurred to Cuban political prisoners, male or female, derived from the circumstances under which their sentences were being served and from the physical and psychological tortures to which they had been subjected.

We could add, due to the high volume they have attained, the deaths of those Cubans, male and female who, not being able to exercise their rights of free passage, dared to leave in whatever manner they could. Since Cuba is an island, they had to improvise rudimentary means of transportation, such as automobile tires and tubes, wooden rafts and other devices, with many of them not reaching their destinations and instead dying in waters of the Straits of Florida through natural causes, starvation, sunburn, thirst or because they were murdered by members of the political police or militia members in charge of watching the seashores.

This led us to proclaim, in 1964, a slogan: "SAVE A LIFE IN CARIBBEAN WATERS", which has served for the commercial or recreation

---

[1]   A.D. = American Declaration of the Rights and Duties of Man.
[2]   U.D. = Universal Declaration of the Rights of Man, U.N.O.

vessels which traversed those waters to be on the alert when cruising near Cuba, whereby we were able to save thousands of lives of men, women and children. We do not want to emphasize the success of our slogan, but to underline the importance that it had to save many human lives, that otherwise could have ended up at the bottom of the sea.

Later on, it was also being done in airplanes through a patriotic and humanitarian organization called "Brethren to the Rescue."

The Inter-American Commission on Human Rights (IACHR) an organism of the Inter-American System, tied to the OAS, created in 1959 precisely due to the situation prevailing in the Caribbean through the presence of a Marxist-Leninist regime, which extended to the Americas of the intervention of an extra-continental power (the Soviet Union) in the internal affairs of this Hemisphere, is in charge of guarding and protecting human rights in the Americas, within the framework of its juridical ordainment and in accordance with the American Declaration of the Rights and Duties of Man and the American Convention on Human Rights, has already prepared and approved SEVEN SPECIAL REPORTS ON HUMAN RIGHTS IN CUBA, and has agreed on preparing another one, that will be the EIGHTH REPORT.

In the First Report from the IACHR, published on May, 1962, with the previous resolutions about violations of human rights in Cuba, it denounced the violation of the right to life. It reiterated the same in another one, the Second, on May, 1963, and in the Third Report, dated April, 1967, this violation of the right to life is reiterated, referring to the "execution wall", adding that "in other cases, the violation of the right to life is effected by agents of armed bodies, with no formulation of a trial." This same pattern of irregular behavior, at times more disguised, has continued being applied up to this date, as the IACHR has maintained on several special reports on violations of human rights in Cuba.

On the Seventh Report, dated October 4, 1983, the IACHR states: "Regarding political prisoners, the circumstances under which they have served their sentences and that may have been the causes of their deaths, it encompasses various situations: Direct and disproportionate executions as disciplinary measures; lack of sufficient medical care, maintaining of the circumstances that brought about a hunger strike on the part of political prisoners and denying the latter minimum medical attention in those circumstances; physical and psychological tortures that led them to suicide, and subjecting them to dangerous situations during the execution of forced labor that triggered fatal accidents."

In conclusion, we can affirm that the right to life, a basic and fundamental right for men and women in Cuba, is subjected to the whim of authorities, with no legal protection and devoid of any moral scruple whatsoever; it is enough that a person will be deemed an enemy of the system, as per Article 62 of the Constitution and the Penal Code in force, and that they consider that due to his/her being a "danger", he/she must be incarcerated or executed.

A.D.: Article II. All persons are equal before the Law, and they have those rights and duties consecrated in this declaration, without distinction by virtue of race, sex, language, creed or any other one.

U.D.: Article II. Every person has all rights and freedoms proclaimed in this Declaration, with no distinction as to race, color, sex, language, religion, political opinion or any other, national origin or social origin, economic status, birth or any other circumstance.

Besides, no distinction shall be made based upon the political, juridical or international situation of the country or territory upon which a person may depend, both when it is an independent country or a territory under trustee administration, not autonomous or subjected to any other limitation of sovereignty.

On Chapter VI, Article 43 of the Socialist Constitution of Cuba, it is said: "Discrimination by reason of race, color, sex, religious or national original is prohibited and is sanctioned by law."

The article of the Socialist Constitution of Cuba above referred to, clearly established discrimination by reason of: Political beliefs. It expressly excludes any other political idea but the Marxist-Leninist one.

It would be too lengthy to list all its articles, but it is sufficient to quote Article 5 of said Constitution, which reads: "Article 5: The Cuban Communist Party, a Martian and Marxist-Leninist one, the organized vanguard of the Cuban nation, is the superior steering force of the society and the state, which organizes and guides the common efforts toward the high purposes of the construction of Socialism and the progress toward a Communist society."

It was approved in the second half of 1992 and maintain the intolerant Marxist-Leninist line, and locks out any possibility of negotiation, change, reform or coexistence in the Americas.

Internally, to Further evaluate the transcendence of those constitutional precepts let us copy what the Cuban Penal Code reads, as it was published on the Cuban Official Gazette dated December 30, 1987: "Title XI: The Dangerous Conditions and Security Measures. Chapter 1: THE DANGEROUS CONDITION. Article 72: It is deemed as a dangerous condition the special proclivity in which a person is for the commission of felonies, as proven by the conduct practiced in express contradiction to the norms of Socialist Morality."

In accordance with this article of the Criminal Code, all Cuban nationals whom the communist regime would like to prosecute, would be covered by this article on the dangerous condition as interpreted by the so-called "Revolutionary Tribunals", made up by Communist, in violation of legal procedures and safeguards established in the civilized world so the person would be punished with the loss of liberty and even life, as it has already happened and continues to happen at the present time.

We do not deem it necessary to mention any more examples as how this institutional violation of the human rights works in practice, since all those who are not ideologically integrated, or politically integrated to the orbit of that integration, would be sure candidates for repression, and even those who were ideologically integrated or politically close, would also be at the mercy of whims, ambitions and acts, always wrong, from those who issue the orders in the highest levels of totalitarianism.

A.D. Article III. Every person is entitled to freely profess a religious conviction and to express and practice it, publicly or privately.

U.D. Article 18. Every person is entitled to freedom of thought, conscience and religion; this right includes the freedom to change religion or belief, as well as the liberty to express his/her religion or belief, individually or collectively, both publicly or privately, through teaching, practice, cult and observance.

The Socialist Constitution of Cuba of 1976 in its Article 54;

"The Socialist State, which bases its activity and teaches the people upon the materialistic scientific conception of the universe, recognizes and guarantees freedom of conscience, the right of each one to profess any religious belief and to practice within respect of the law, the cult of his/her preference. The activities of religious institutions shall be regulated by law."

"It is illegal and punishable to impose faith or religious belief to the Revolution, to education or to the compliance with the duties to work, to defend the nation with arms, to reverse its symbols and the other duties established by the Constitution." (This is what they have been doing in Cuba during the last 34 years and continue to do today).

Through this constitutional norm, the presumed right that it is said guaranteed is instead violated institutionally. The Government still atheist and materialistic, anything opposed to it is punishable. Besides, it leaves to the arbitrariness of the rulers the task of interpreting when religious beliefs are opposed to the Marxist-Leninist Revolution.

The Constitution itself stipulates that "the Socialist State, that bases its activity and teaches the people upon the materialistic conception of the universe" leaves no margin of religious tolerance, except that which could be convenient for the tactical interests of communist propaganda abroad, to pretend a respect that it does not practice. Thus it has happened in practice, both in Cuba and in almost all communist-subjugated nations, and we say "almost all", because in other places even this propaganda pretext has been eliminated.

In Cuba, under the disposition of said text, believers have been discriminated against as to the holding of public office at all levels of the State. They are also denied parents' rights to decide about the kind of education that they would like to give their children, both religious and moral.

This Article 5 emphasizes the dogmatic nature of teaching, framed within the Marxist-Leninist delimitations.

With the regime having control of all State resources, all media and all teaching, any possibility to effect any kind of effective religious education is eliminated, and its practice makes people into second- or third-class citizens.

Since 1960, the Cuban communist regime began an accelerated drive to dismount and render inoperable the religious structures of the country. The Catholic Church, as well as the Protestant and Jewish religious, saw their cadres diminished, their schools closed, their media suppressed and their believers marginated from civic and public activities.

In 1961, 131 Catholic priests and church ministers, a Bishop among them, were forcibly taken away from their religious centers and shipped on the freighter "Covadonga" to Spain, without allowing them to carry their belongings, through fear that they could carry documents which denounced the monstrous religious persecution that was taking place in Cuba.

When communism seized power in Cuba in 1959, there were 12,500 Jews in Cuba, out of which 12,000 have left the island, and around 500 remain, without the spiritual assistance of any Cuba-based Rabbi.

Jehovah's witnesses have also been persecuted, and some even sent to the firing squads. The communists have been especially merciless with the latter, although repression has been generalized.

Father Miguel Loredo, O.F.M., who was falsely accused of covering up for a pilot who tried to escape from Cuba, was sentenced to 15 years in prison, forcing him to perform mandatory labor. Father Loredo served 10 years in prison and has testified in exile about religious persecution and the horrors of the Cuban political prisons.

There were created in Cuba the so-called UMAP camps, where thousands of Cubans were shipped to do forced labor, among them many priests. We could point out many instances, but that of Msgr. Alfredo Petit, the director of a Catholic seminary, whom Pope John Paul II has appointed to be Auxiliary Bishop of La Habana, on November 1991, would be sufficient.

Persecution for religious reasons has continued unabated, and it will continue while the communist regime remains in power, because religion is intrinsically inimical to the atheist and materialist Marxist-Leninist.

A.D. Article IV. Every person is entitled to freedom of investigation, opinion, expression and divulgent of thought by any means.

U.D. On Article 18 of the Universal Declaration of Human Rights, already mentioned, it is stipulated that: "Every person is entitled to freedom of thought..."

In the Socialist Constitution of Cuba, Article 53, the following is stipulated: "It is recognized for citizens freedom of expression and press, in accordance with the purposes of the Socialist society. Material conditions for its exercise are given by the fact that the press, radio, television, movies and other communication media are state or social properties and cannot be the object, in any case, of private property, which assures its use for the exclusive service of the working people and the interest of society."

The subordination that the Cuban Constitution establishes for the exercise of the right to freedom of expression is total, directed to "the purposes of the Socialist Society."

We must underline that this precept does not deal with limitations established in other legal ordinations about public order, morals, etc. The suppression of that freedom for citizens is total and absolute here.

Since the communist regime is the owner of all media: Press, radio, television, movies, etc., the citizen has no way to express himself/herself and, should he/she do it outside of the regime, would be severely punished.

In order to supplement this constitutional norm, the Penal Code in force in Cuba disposes, in its Article 108, the following:

1. A sentence of incarceration will be imposed, from one to eight years, to whoever will:

   a. Incite against the social order, international solidarity or the Socialist State, through verbal or written propaganda, or in any other manner.

   b. Prepare, distribute or hold any propaganda of the nature mentioned in the previous clause.

   c. Whoever propagates false news or malicious predictions, tending to cause alarm or unrest in the population, or public disorder, will be liable for a sentence of incarceration between one and four years.

   d. If for the execution of the deeds mentioned in the prior clauses, mass-communication media are utilized, the sentence shall be from seven to fifteen years of prison.

e.   Whoever will permit the use of mass-communication media referred to in the previous clause, shall incur in a sentence of one to four years of prison.

Article 121 of the same legal body reads:

Whoever will propagate false news with the purpose of disturbing international peace, or of endangering the prestige or the credit of the Cuban State, or its good relationship with another State, shall incur a sanction of imprisonment from one to four years.

Article 160 of the Penal Code reads:

1.   Whoever will threaten, slander, defame, insult, offend or in any manner will affront or humiliate, in writing or verbally, in his/her dignity or decorum, any authority, public official, or their agents or aides in the exercise of their functions or by reason of them, shall incur a sanction of imprisonment from three to nine months or a fine from one-hundred to two-hundred seventy quotas, or both.

2.   If the deed contemplated in the previous clause is performed with regard to the President of the Council of State, the President of the National Assembly of the Popular Power, the members of the Council of State or of the Cabinet, or the Deputies to the National Assembly of the Popular Power, the sanction shall be imprisonment from six months to three years."

Article 39 of the Constitution stipulates:

"The State guides, fosters and promotes education, culture and sciences in all of their manifestations. In its educational and cultural policy, it follows the principles listed below:

a)   It bases its educational and cultural policies upon the scientific conception of the world, established and developed by Marxism-Leninism.

b)   Education is a function of the State. Consequently, the learning centers are the property of the State.

61

Compliance with the educational function is a task in which all of society participates and is based upon the conclusions of contributions of science and in a closer relationship of the study with life, work and production.

c) Promotion of the patriotic and communist formation of the new generations and the preparation of children, youngsters and adults for social life.

d) Artistic creation is free, as long as its contents shall not contradict the Revolution."

Etc...

When dealing with the mass-communication media, Article 105 of the Programmatic Platform of the Communist Party reads as follows:

"The Party prepares a systemic orientation and attention for the mass-communication media, and it shall promote an enthusiastic and creative participation by all workers who labor in them, relying in the communists and upon the activity of the labor union movement, journalists' unions and writers' unions, with the purpose of attaining that radio, television, written press and movies accomplish, in an increasingly efficient manner, their functions in the political, ideological, cultural, scientific/technical and esthetic education of the population."

The application of this legislation and of the programmatic guides of the Communist Party within the parameters of the Marxist-Leninist doctrine, render freedom of expression totally inoperable, as well as the freedom of the press, artistic freedom and educational freedom.

A.D. Article VIII of the American Declaration of the Rights and Duties of Man:

"Every person is entitled to locate his/her residence in the territory of the State of which he/she is a national, to travel freely through it and to not leave it out for his/her will."

U.D. Article 13 of the Universal Declaration of Human Rights:

1.   "Every person has the right to freely travel and choose his/her residence in the territory of a State.

2.   Every person has the right to leave any country, including his/her own, and to return to his/her country."

These rights are inherent to the human person; they are elementary rights that are included in almost all of the constitutions and in all of the human rights declarations.

<u>That right to residence and transit is not mentioned in the socialist constitution, which constitutes an omission</u> that violates a human right granted and expressly pointed out in all precepts related with the subject in all civilized nations.

We believe that it is intentional omission, intended to limit, hamper and in many cases totally suppress that freedom, which is inherent to the human being.

In Cuba, those laws that control immigration, emigration and travels are included, in their major proportion, within the Immigration Law and its regulations, as well as in the Foreign Nationals' Law and its regulations.

We already know how those Marxist-Leninist governments that have subjugated many countries, which bear the misfortune of enduring those regimes, limit and punish people who try to leave. The Berlin Wall was the best example of impediment for free passage of East Germans towards the other part of their territory, arbitrarily separated.

In Cuba, leaving the island-nation has become an odyssey, as it has happened in the Soviet Union with Jews. The communist regime takes advantage of the departures and arrivals of Cuban citizens, makes a mockery of all legal regulations existing in civilized nations, and so on.

Whoever states in Cuba his/her wish to go abroad, is deemed as a dangerous enemy of the regime; these persons are deprived of their jobs, their rationing cards, instructions for their children and any other protection, and they are also subjected to acts of repudiation, an offensive and criminal practice.

Those Cubans who risk leaving clandestinely, because of every other possibility having been exhausted, know that their lives are endangered; they can find death because of the attempt or lose their "freedom", in the process compromising their own families, who would have to detest the "fugitive" in order to avoid reprisals.

Permits to leave the country are punitive. In more than several instances, previously alerted mobs with adequate training and every resource at their disposal, will take charge of making their lives unbearable, for those who may have stated their intention to leave, be it personally or with the family nucleus, and even more if this attempt is a collective one. In the latter instance, all the wrath of the fanatics befalls on them, as the case was with those who took refuge in the Peruvian Embassy and with the Mariel Exodus. We will mention these again upon dealing with the right to asylum.

In general terms, when a person states in Cuba his/her intention to leave the country, that person knows that he/she will lose his/her job; that food will be scarce because their rationing card are taken away and that they will become "enemies" of the regime. They are subjected to questioning capable of breaking their nervous systems. They receive notices of departure for a certain date, but these are postponed time and time again, until the "enemies" have been sufficiently punished. This has been taking place since the beginning of the communist repression.

To move within the country, certain requirements have to be met. Formerly, the person had to get a "transit card." At any rate, the so-called committees for the Defense of the Revolution, which are really "watchdog organizations", will be in charge of reporting the presence of any person who is not a resident of the area, whenever one of these arrives in their jurisdiction. The person will have to appear before the Committee, tell them what is the purpose of his/her being there and how long he/she is going to stay. He/she will be required to tell the "responsible comrades" in the Committee.

Surveillance is close for everyone and everything that moves in Cuba, especially persons.

Changing residence is a very difficult endeavor, because the State is the owner of everything.

A.D. In Article XXIII of the American Declaration of the Rights and Duties of Man, it is stipulated that:

"Every person is entitled to the private property that is pertinent to the indispensable needs of a decent life, and which contributes to maintain the dignity of the person and the home."

U.D. Article 17 of the Universal Declaration of Human Rights reads as follows:

1) Every person is entitled to property, individually and collectively.

2) No person shall be arbitrarily deprived of his/her property.

Articles 14 and 15 of the Socialist Constitution of Cuba read:

14. In the Republic of Cuba, there prevails the socialist system of economics, based upon the socialist ownership of the whole people over the means of production, and upon the suppression of the exploitation of man by man.

15. Socialist State property, which is the ownership of all the people, is established irreversibly upon lands that do not belong to small farmers or cooperatives made up by the same; upon the subsoil, the mines, marine resources both natural and alive within the area of its sovereignty, the woods, the waters, the means of transportation and any other enterprises, banks, installations and wealth that have been nationalized and expropriated from the imperialists, landholders and bourgeois, as well as on the people's farms, factories, enterprises and economic, social, cultural and sports installations that have been built, fomented or acquired by the State, and those built, fomented or acquired in the future.
et sequitur...

This State property does not have anything to do with the ownership of cooperatives that operate in the Western World, since the members of Cuban cooperatives have no right to the disposition of their products, nor to the fruits of their labor, since the Socialist State disposes of everything.

The euphemism with which these articles refer to "the property of the whole people" must not be taken at face value, since the people does not participate in their management; this is done by the State's bureaucracy; the products of those cooperatives end up in the hands of the "State", that is, the "new class" of communist leaders, that are not accountable to anybody in the people.

The production of small farms does not belong, either, to the falsely designated as "small farmers", who in reality are but workers exploited by the State. The products of the work of these farmers go to the State, which performs the marketing and gives those farmers a minimum share of the fruits of their labors. Anyone who disposes of the fruits of his/her labor can be punished.

State property, in Cuba, includes all the means of production and all services.

The Constitution itself, in the Article 15 listed above, and in Articles 18, 39 and others, takes care of specifying the extent of the State property in construction, internal commerce (wholesale and retail), fisheries, health services, hotels, restaurants, night clubs, movie theaters, and all other recreation and touristic centers.

Almost all means of production began to be confiscated in 1960 through "nationalization", "expropriation" and "recovery."

What the so-called "agrarian reforms" of 1959 and 1963 really intended was the collectivization of all lands. In the late 1960's, even the street booths for the sale of food and other products were confiscated and incorporated to State property. The confiscation even reached craftsmanship activities performed in a family setting, revealing the true nature of the regime that, as in ancient Greece, rejects the basic elements of technology.

It can be said, without any doubt or mistake, that private property in its entirety, such as it is understood in the Western World, has disappeared in Cuba, and that the so-called "Socialist State", made up by the "new class", is the absolute owner of everything. Nowadays, property in Cuba has a State and bureaucratic function, not a social function.

The alleged owners of the dwellings that they inhabit cannot lease, mortgage or encumber it, and they can only be inherited by a person who has no other real property. The alleged owners of the dwellings are really less than tenants, since their right to lease is subjected to the dictate of the totalitarian State's bureaucracy. Since 1970, the hierarchy of the totalitarian State resolved to postpone indefinitely the "awarding" of the right of ownership for the dwellings, alleging ideological and economic reasons, with which they have left in a precarious situation those who presently inhabit them.

THE RIGHT TO WORK

A.D.   Article XIV of the American Declaration reads:

"Every person is entitled to work in dignified circumstances and to pursue freely his/her vocation,   as permitted by the existing employment opportunities."

"Each working person is entitled to receive a remuneration that, regarding his/her capability and expertise,   will assure him/her a convenient level of life for himself/herself and the family."

U.D.   Article 23 of the Universal Declaration stipulates:

1.   "Every person is entitled to work,   to freely elect his/her work,   to equitable circumstances for working,   and to protection against unemployment."

2.   "Every working person is entitled to an equitable and satisfactory remuneration that will assure him/her,   as well as his/her family,   an existence in accordance with human dignity and which shall be complemented,   if need be,   by any other means of social protection.

3.   Every person is entitled,   without discrimination,   to an equal salary for equal work.

4.   Every person is entitled to organize labor unions and to be a member of a labor union for the defense of his/her interest.

The American Declaration,   in its Article XXII,   supplements the last clause of the Universal Declaration,   when it reads: "Every person is entitled to assemble peacefully,   with other persons,   in order to promote,   exercise and protect his/her legitimate interests or a political,   economic,   religious, social,   cultural,   professional,   labor or any other nature."

The Socialist Constitution of Cuba,   in its Article 9,   Clause 8, points out: "As people's power at the service of the people proper,   it guarantees ... that there shall not be any man or woman,   capable of working, who will not have an opportunity of obtaining employment with which he/she may contribute to the purposes of society and the fulfillment of his/her own needs."

Article 45 of the same Constitution reads: "Work is a right in the Socialist Society, a duty and a motive of honor for each citizen.

The emphasis in the Socialist Constitution is made upon the alleged society and not upon the individual or the family, nor in accordance with his/her needs. The sacrifice of the human person is not his/her contribution to society, but that from the society to the individual (really the totalitarian state).

All achievements and benefits that the Cuban labor movement had attained, perhaps the most advanced one in the hemisphere, have been eliminated in the communist regime of Cuba.

The Cuban Confederation of Workers (Spanish acronym C.T.C.) had achieved, when communism seized power, to be the strongest pillar of the labor movement, and it had significantly contributed to the economic, social and political development of the country. The C.T.C. enjoyed total independence and freedom. The Cuban labor movement was the most advanced one in the Americas, and its achievements on behalf of workers were the best in the Americas.

The communist regime eliminated the right of free syndication and association of workers. Also, the rights to strike, to petition and to collective bargaining have been eliminated, and workers are subjected to the guardianship of the Communist Party.

The right established by Article XIV of the American Declaration, mentioned above, has been suppressed. Said article stipulates the right of every person to pursue his/her vocation freely. The freedom to choose employment has been eliminated in Cuba, since the State is the only employer; it is the State which determines what employment each person should have and, in that context, the State subordinates employment not to the needs of the person and of his/her family, but to the demands of the economy and of the society. The elimination of that right for workers is evident.

This is not limited only to manual workers; the State points out, through a State planning, how many physicians, engineers, architects, dentists, professors, etc., there will be; we have omitted lawyers because that profession has been suppressed for practical purposes, as we know it in the Western World.

The communist regime gives priority to ideological considerations upon choosing among workers. We have already seen how the opponents of the regime are marginated and displaced without any right to file any claim whatsoever, and without any other opportunity to work but for the State and those enterprises controlled by it. This leads to either simulated or true ideological participation, due to the indispensable need to work.

Through the so-called "vagrancy law," enacted in 1971, the possibilities of working outside of the State's sphere were even limited much further.

Despite that, working outside the State's orbit and parallel to it has been developing, albeit confronting all risks involved in it.

Because all of those regulations and the regime's orientation, work is subordinated to the totalitarian State, with no easy way out for workers.

Those, within the Cuban communist regime, are not free to change jobs nor to choose employment. He/she will work where the State will indicate, under the conditions imposed by it, without any right to any claim, lest he/she be accused of being a "counter-revolutionary"; with all consequences that such consideration may bring for him/her and the family.

The Socialist Constitution establishes mandatory work, that is, work as an obligation, and this duty in that regime overrules the right to work. Such duty is set by the State, it is not left to the will of workers. Lack of compliance with it has punishable connotations. The so-called "voluntary work" is included in said duty, and it is but another deceit.

Workers are obligated to perform, correctly and faithfully, all tasks assigned them, not being able to claim anything against them. That performance is subordinated to the interpretation given by the person "responsible" for the shop or working center, and the human factors derived from relationships between persons exert and influence upon that interpretation.

Workers are obligated to accept, without any right to complain, the "working discipline" that in many instances is set arbitrarily by the "responsible person" in charge of said work, who is endowed with ample authority.

Tacitly, the "responsible person," or the manager, represents the State's interests, those of the whole people and his/her powers are almost unlimited.

THE ADDED VALUE

One of the basic elements of the Marxist-Leninist doctrine is the Surplus Value, Added Value or Goodwill, which according to Marx's definition is that part of the workers' production which went to the hands of the capitalist entrepreneur. In the Marxist-Leninist regime, that element is transferred to the State and absorbed by the "new class," made up by the new exploiters of the workers, in accordance with their own doctrine, to nurture an hypertrophy and inept bureaucracy.

To go into the analysis of Surplus Value would be too extensive, and it is not the objective of this book.

Finally, to that respect, we must add that workers cannot demand any participation in that Surplus Value, nor request any wage increase, nor perform any collective drive to achieve improvements or social benefits, since they would be classified as "enemies of the regime." Not only are they forbidden to have their rights, but they are also prohibited from complaining about the dispossession.

THE RIGHT TO PETITION

Workers, as the rest of the population, are denied the right to petition, comprised in Article XXIV of the American Declaration, that reads:

"Every person has the right to submit respectful petitions to any competent authority, be it by reason of general interest, or because of a private interest, and to obtain a speedy resolution."

A Cuban national who petitioned to learn whether he could register a Movement Pro-Marti, was imprisoned and sentenced to several years in confinement.

There is no possibility to exercise this right, because every order from the authorities must be complied with. No person can make any kind of petition that could be, tacitly or expressly, against the Revolution or against the Marxist-Leninist doctrine.

THE RIGHT OF PROTECTION AGAINST THE ARBITRARY DETENTION

A.D. Article XXV of the American Declaration reads:

"No person can be deprived of his/her freedom but in those cases and according to the procedures established by preexisting laws."

"No person can be detained for lack of compliance with obligations of a merely civil nature."

"Any person deprived of freedom has the right to have a Judge verify, without delay, the legality of that measure and to be judged without unjustified delay or, on the contrary, to be set free. Said person has also the right to a human treatment during his/her deprivation of freedom."

U.D. Article 9 of the Universal Declaration reads:

"No person shall be arbitrarily detained, imprisoned or expatriated."

The 1940 Constitution of Cuba, democratically approved, guaranteed all the fundamental rights of the human person. This Constitution was immediately amended after the communist regime seized power in Cuba. It was replaced by the so-called "Fundamental Law" of February 7, 1959. Already on January 30, 1959, the Council of Ministers, on which legislative powers had been invested, modified Articles 27, 29, 196 and 197 of the 1940 Constitution; through that amendment a long list of individual guarantees were suspended, fundamental rights among which there was the duty to have a detained person appear before a Judge within 72 hours of having been detained; the right of "habeas corpus" was suspended, and the infamous peoples' Courts were created. Although it was said that the suspension of those rights and freedoms would be only for 90 days, a new amendment to the Constitution, on November, 1969, perpetuated the permanency of those changes, that were fundamentally adverse to individual liberty.

None of the procedural guarantees, nor those freedoms enshrined in the American Declaration or the United Nations' Universal Declaration of Human Rights, exist today.

To add insult to injury, detainees are not taken before a competent authority within the 72 hours from their arrests, but months and even years elapse without any news of their whereabouts and, should anyone insist on finding out, that person could pay for the temerity with his/her own life.

Disappearances of political prisoners have been frequent since 1959 to date; it has thus been stated by the Inter-American Commission on Human Rights (IACHR) in seven reports about violations of human rights in Cuba.

Said Commission has declared that "a cruel, inhuman and degrading treatment is given to Cuban political prisoners." And this kind of treatment, with greater or lesser intensity, continues being applied to Cuban political prisoners.

"The integrity and safety of the human person is constantly violated in Cuba, from the inception of the (communist) regime." The Inter-American Commission on Human Rights has stated thus in several reports and resolutions.

In its Seventh Report, the IACHR has declared that Cuban political prisoners are locked up in "drawers," a tiny space where two or more persons are kept, despite the fact that there is only room for one. Down there, without even being able to move, they must take care of their physical necessities and they receive a very scarce feeding.

They are also locked up in "walled-up cells" (tapiadas) in the somber Boniato prison, near Santiago de Cuba; in Guanajay, near the city of Havana, where female political prisoners are incarcerated.

Other diverse manners of physical and psychological tortures are applied to them.

THE RIGHT TO POLITICAL ASYLUM

One of the fundamental concepts of Public International Law, a proud one for Latin-America, is the right to political asylum, born in the Americas, and which is practiced in Latin-American nations.

This right to political asylum was born precisely in Havana, Cuba, in the American Conference of 1928. It was speedily ratified and took effect, and it is practiced and respected in all countries of Latin-America.

The present Cuban regime has repeatedly violated this right, preventing its enforcement by surrounding with armed police officers the embassies that enjoy the right of extraterritoriality. Because of it, nobody could enter an embassy, except by risking his/her life and those of the officers guarding the embassy in question, as it has already happened in several opportunities.

Three Cuban nationals, Eduardo Herrera Diaz, Feliciano Ramirez Batista and Pedro Betancourt Baños, took haven in the Peruvian Embassy at Havana, dodging the surveillance of the guards. This took place in 1980, and they have been there for fourteen years and have been denied safe-conduct.

A similar thing was done in Gen. Odria in Peru regarding Victor Raúl Haya de la Torre, who sought asylum in the Embassy of Colombia in Lima. That was a big scandal at that time.

Article 249 of the Cuban Penal Code has declared the right to political asylum as a felony in Cuba.

To illustrate our statement about the impediments to the exercise of the right to political asylum, we would like to recall that, in 1980, the Cuban communist regime retired all guards from the Peruvian Embassy at Havana. As soon as the Cuban people learned that there were no guards at that embassy, and that they could seek asylum there, a stampede ensued and 10,500 men, women and children went inside the embassy grounds, that were not capable of holding such a massive influx of persons. It was not possible for any others to get in there. That was proof of the discontent and disgust of the Cuban people for the regime it repudiates.

A great deal of difficulty was arrayed against those who sought asylum in said embassy. The Cuban communist regime offered safe conduct to

2,500 of them, saying that they could wait for their time to leave in their own homes, where they would be more comfortable. Most of them have not left yet, others were imprisoned, still others have disappeared and all of them have been deemed "non-persons," enemies of the regime, with all of the serious implications that such a classification entails.

As a consequence of the massive asylum in the Peruvian Embassy, the communist regime tried to mitigate the effects of that diplomatic setback, at the same time a political calamity. The regime said that everyone who wanted to leave could do so, and opened the port of Mariel, in the northern coast of Pinar del Rio province, to that effect. A total of 125,000 people went into exile through that port, among whom the communist regime infiltrated subversive agents, narcotics traffickers, criminals and deranged persons, in order to harm the reputations of the Cuban patriots who went to exile through that port.

THE CUBAN EXILE

The Cuban exile since 1959 to date is close to a million and a half persons, the largest exodus recorded in the history of the Americas, and one of the largest in the world. A 10% of the Cuban population is in exile in several countries of the Americas, especially the United States; there are also many in Europe, Asia and Africa. They are scattered throughout the whole world.

The vast majority of Cubans remaining in the island would also go into exile if they could, but since Cuba is an island, it becomes very difficult for its citizens to escape the oppression of the communist regime.

The increasing number of exiled persons, undoubtedly, is an obvious demonstration of the Cuban people's repudiation towards the Marxist-Leninist regime.

AMENDMENTS TO THE CUBAN PENAL CODE

Our repeated denunciations, over almost three decades, about the institutional violation of human rights and on the human violation in the communist regimes, have had some partial effect in Cuba and the Soviet Union.

On October 13, 1987, the Cuban Minister of Justice announced that the modification of the Penal Code was being studied, in order to introduce some amendments to the same (about institutional violations of human rights, we would underline.)

The same official said that, after 30 years, the Revolution could already be more flexible, because opposition was not so intense and sanctions should be lesser, some of the violations of the code could be eliminated from its text, albeit others would be added, aiming at the same ends.

The Minister alluded to the necessity of introducing some elements of "detypification and pardon" (elimination of the criminal nature). He also said that there were some infractions that carried very severe sanctions and it was necessary to reduce the latter.

He added that many other infractions against the economy would be included in the new Penal Code.

PRESENT CHANGES IN THE SOVIET UNION AND THEIR IMPORTANCE AS TO HUMAN RIGHTS AND, ESPECIALLY, TO THE INSTITUTIONAL VIOLATION

Changes in the Soviet Union are not only of a structural and nominal nature, but they transcend the philosophic, doctrinary and ideological fields, albeit they are still in the path of institutionalizing them, and even more distant from complying with them in accordance with the statement. There is a great distance between stating and norming, especially in such a difficult field to define as that which was encompassed, for the last 74 years, under Marxism-Leninism. That is why we must take inventory of the good intentions and the preliminary agreements that have taken place.

We had mentioned the changes that the Soviet Union was intending to make in the Penal Code and the Constitution, before the great changes that have now taken place and, especially, after the failed "coup d'état" in August, 1991.

The Soviet Constitution is still in force, within the parameters of the previous system and as a representation of the same, until a Constitutional Assembly will be convened to write a new one. When will this occur? Nobody, inside or outside of the Soviet Union, would dare to venture an accurate date, but the purpose exists and so does the necessity.

We must underline that some amendments have taken effect, such as the one regarding the elimination of the position of Vice-President, as well as a statement related to human rights that would substantially alter the juridical structure in this field.

Before entering to consider the scope of these amendments and changes, we deem it convenient to reproduce here as the situation was before and what changes were proposed then, and finally we will point out the declaration of human rights and what this could mean for the present and future of the Union of Soviet Sovereign Republics, whose name was also the subject of a change.

On Economic Infractions

The economic violation, which is typical of communist-subjugated countries, would reach its maximum development in the Soviet Union and

Cuba, as well as its highest sanctions, since the economy is the backbone of the system and the largest failure that reflects negatively on the economic and social rights of their citizens.

AMENDMENTS TO THE SOVIET PENAL CODE

The Soviet Minister of Justice, almost simultaneously with the Cuban case, stated that his government was getting ready to amend the Soviet Penal Code, especially regarding the punishments established for certain infractions that carried internal exile (to Siberia) and the death penalty.

He said that the maximum sentence for internal exile would be reduced to ten years and that only some violations would be punished with the death penalty. Even now, after the crumbling of the communist regime, there are political prisoners comprised in this category.

Internal exile, a punishment applied in the Soviet Union since Pushkin to Sakharov to the enemies of the regime, has caused numerous deaths, mutilations and physical and mental destruction of male and female political prisoners, whose human rights have been violated, both in the institutional and in the human orders, as it has been verified.

It is reported that among the articles of the Soviet Penal Code that are slated for modification, there are Nos. 72 and 190-1. The modifications or reforms of the said code could reach other articles that have been frequently utilized in the Soviet Union during the recent past.

Whatever the scope of the modifications could be, there is something certain that transcends the juridical order established there, and it is that it has been discovered that human rights are institutionally violated in their legislation, since these violations are intrinsical to the communist system. Even today, the communist doctrine has not completely disappeared.

THE CONSTITUTION OF THE SOVIET UNION: INSTITUTIONAL VIOLATION

In the Soviet Union, as in every other nation subjected to Marxist-Leninist regime, a REGRESSIVE TRANSCULTURATION takes place, that is, a return to the pagan stage of social organization, even more serious than polytheist civilizations, because the former is atheist, militantly atheist and materialistic. This is the negation of God, the suppression of all relationship with God, of every invocation to God, and an anthropocentric materialistic cosmovision is expressly declared, countering the theocentric cosmovision enshrined in those constitutions that invoke God.

The Soviet Constitution mirrors, in the constitutional norming, the whole structure of the system, based upon the ideological guidelines from DAS KAPITAL, by Karl Marx, and Lenin's contributions to them.

Article 6 of the Soviet Constitution reads: "The guidance and strength of the Soviet society and of its political system is the Communist Party. The Communist Party determines the course of the internal and external policies of the Union of Soviet Socialist Republics; directs the constructive work of the Soviet people, imparts systematically and theoretically the plans to substantiate the nature of the struggle towards the victory of communism.

Although the Communist Party has been declared as dissolved, many of its consequences are still present.

The Soviet Union did not conceal its true intentions nor the basic elements of its struggle for the implementation of communism.

Article 39 of the Soviet Constitution is very similar to Article 61 of the Cuban Constitution. Said Article 39 states that whatever Soviet citizens will make with their rights and liberty, shall never be done to the detriment of society or the State. That is, they will never be able to exercise their rights against socialism or communism. Exactly the same as in Cuba.

All Soviet citizens are constitutionally obligated to honor and defend socialism; they must observe a standard of conduct in accordance with socialist parameters.

Because of Lenin's identification of State-Government-Power, the system absorbs all rights, that citizens will not be able to exercise against the Totalitarian State, whose rights do not emanate from popular sovereignty.

We cannot mix up the enumeration of certain rights in the Soviet Constitution with those others that are listed in the Western nations' constitutions, since in the former case its exercise is totally controlled by the ruling class, the "new class," and it is up to members of the latter to say when and how those rights can be exercised without hampering the course of the Socialist State and the construction of communism. All of this renders those rights ineffective; they only appear on paper, but are absent from practice in Soviet life. And this is so not only for those born in the Soviet Union, but also for all of those nations or human groups forcibly incorporated into the so-called Union of Soviet Socialist Republics, which is no such thing.

The Soviet Constitution is made up of 174 articles and constitutional regulations. Many of those have been written there as a way to feed "disinformation" to the Western World, but with no value nor effect in the practice of human rights on Soviet territory.

In the Soviet Union, only the existence of one party is constitutionally guaranteed: That of the Communist Party (now apparently dissolved).

Education, totally controlled by the State, shall be Marxist-Leninist. Now, with its "Socialist" variant, it continues to develop within these parameters.

Freedoms of expression, thought, assembly, unionization or education are all absent, such as we know them in the West. (Modifications have been extensive.)

Article 52 of the Soviet Constitution guarantees all citizens the right to profess any religion, as it is in Cuba. But since the State has an atheist and materialistic nature, religion shall not counter the State nor the construction of communism.

Religious freedom has begun to function through the virtual regression of communism. It is not sufficient, per se, for the establishment of religious freedom, after 74 years of a massive materialistic isolation.

Religious activities are very limited, it is still punishable, albeit not totally, in order not to antagonize religious organizations in the world, and while communism will not be extensive to all nations, as its objectives are.

Several worship places are open, but they have been condemned in its majority. Religious organizations lack the necessary resources to divulgate their religious ideas, because all of those resources are under State control. But temples are being opened.

Practitioners of religion in the Soviet Union will run the same fate as those who practice it in Cuba: They will lose their right to intermediate and higher education; they will not be eligible for public positions; they will not be entitled to well-paid jobs and their supply of food will be rationed, directly or indirectly. In those establishments devoted to medical attention, members of the Party will have priority, as well as in the case of housing and transportation (automobiles, etc.).

Regarding the freedoms of expression and thought, Article 50 of the USSR's Socialist Constitution states that, in accordance with the interests of the people, and in order to strengthen and develop the socialist system, the USSR guarantees the right to freedom of expression, press, assembly, street processions and public demonstrations.

There must be no confusion with this Article, since its objectives are very clear: These rights are only granted in order to develop the socialist system; anyone who uses them against the system shall be punished, as it has happened from 1917 to the present time in the Soviet Union.

There are no limits in the Socialist Constitution of the USSR for the power of the State, that will be all-powerful and shall have all rights; there is no guarantee for the inalienable and imprescriptible human rights, nor for the development of the dignity of the human person and respect for same. There is an institutional violation of human rights. It is "legal" to violate human rights there. (This is in the process of being abolished.)

There is no rule of law in the Soviet Union, as it is defined in the Western World. The Rule of Law shall be subjected to the mandates of the Party, albeit with more disguising than in Cuba. (The rule of law is in the process of being re-established.)

The division of powers, as defined by Montesquieu, does not exist in the Soviet Union. The Executive Power controls everything, and in turn it is controlled by the acting Secretary General of the Communist Party. (Some structural changes have modified this.)

Communism has an ANTHROPOCENTRIC COSMOVISION, as opposed to democracy, which has a THEOCENTRIC COSMOVISION.

All of this, many in the Soviet Union say, belongs to the recent past, which many want to erase and forget, but a lot of it is still in force, if not in political declarations and programs, at least in the structure of thought, in the adherence to the ideology that they have practiced thus far, even those who say that they are against it. They were formed, since their birth up to the present, within that polluting atmosphere.

Presently, in the Soviet Union, the Council of the Republics and the Council of the Union can make changes in the Constitution. Both must adopt their resolutions jointly and apply them in the respective republics and, as it is natural, that application will not be uniform nor would it have the same scope in one as in the other, because of which its observance must be watched.

Changes in the Constitution have to be submitted, in the first place, to a vote by the Council of the Union, and later on by the Council of the Republics.

After both legislative councils have voted regarding any change, this must be voted upon in the republics through their legislatures. Only after it has been approved by all of the republics, it will have the strength of law.

A very important issue in the legislative aspect has not been established: The relationships of the republics among them and with the central power.

The Congress of People's Deputies, in its last assembly on September 5, 1991, approved a DECLARATION OF HUMAN RIGHTS IN THE SOVIET UNION, as an amendment to the Constitution, with 31 new articles.

We can summarize the substantial compendium of said declaration as follows:

"NO GROUP, PARTY OR STATE INTEREST SHALL BE ABOVE THE INTERESTS OF THE HUMAN PERSON."

That is, among other basic elements, the difference between a communist regime and a democratic regime: The treatment given to the human person.

Up until now, many things have changed in the Soviet Union; some of them substantially and others with an entity value but, in our opinion, the most important and one which would typify the change of the system, should there be one, is the Institutionalization of this statement as the new foundation of the reformed or substantially changed system.

While in a communist totalitarian regime, such as that in the Soviet Union, from its inception in 1917, and that of Cuba since 1959, human beings are subordinated to the group, to the party and to the State, with men and women helpless vis-à-vis the Totalitarian State, in democratic regimes the human person keeps his/her rights, which are inalienable and imprescriptible, that must be protected and guaranteed by the State.

We have documented all of this for over three decades, as the INSTITUTIONAL VIOLATION and the HUMAN VIOLATION of HUMAN RIGHTS, they are the foundations of the "BENEDI DOCTRINE," recognized in the Americas and Europe and that now, with the events that have taken place in the Soviet Union and the communist-subjugated nations of Eastern Europe. It has been proven without any doubt that the "BENEDI DOCTRINE," is the foundation of democratic regimes and of all those in which the human person, in his/her most ample concept, in his/her dignity and freedom, in which all of his/her rights are respected and protected. And, likewise, it constitutes a negation of communist regimes.

HIGH COMMISSIONER FOR HUMAN RIGHTS APPROVED AT WORLD LEVEL FOR UNITED NATIONS

The United Nations, in its general assembly meeting held on December 20, 1993, approved by a vote of 184 members in favor, which is tantamount to unanimity, the creation of the position of High Commissioner for Human Rights with an attributed rank similar to that of United Nations Adjunct Secretary, a great step forward in the lengthy and difficult process of defending and guaranteeing the enforcement and unlimited respect for human rights in the world.

This important event comes 48 years after the creation of the United Nations, and 45 years after the approval of the two most important multilateral statements on human rights in the world: The American Declaration of the Rights and Duties of Man, approved on April, 1948, in Bogota, South America, and the United Nations Universal Declaration of Human Rights, approved on December, 1948, in Paris. Approval could not be obtained earlier due to the predominance of tragic philosophical, ideological, political and topical currents known by all, which prevented it. Now the environment has increasingly improved and there is more room for the "habitat" of human rights.

A propitious juridical and institutional framework has been created now to establish the strongest possible foundations for the enforcement, guarantee and exercise of human rights in their dual dimension: The Institutional Dimension and the Human Dimension, both within the context of our doctrine, spelled out in this book.

We shall encounter large difficulties and problems in the process of consolidating and implementing the functions of the High Commissioner for Human Rights and, especially, to attain that the high responsibilities of this commissioner shall be, as we believe they ought to be, compatible with those of the Rapporteur appointed by the Human Rights Commission of the United Nations. The appointment of the High Commissioner for Human Rights at the United Nations does not imply, in any manner whatsoever, neither the elimination nor the curtailment of the functions ascribed to the Rapporteur, which in our opinion are complementary.

The following are some of the possible difficulties which could be encountered:

1) The appointment of the High Commissioner. The selection of the person for such a high position will be a rather difficult task, since such an official will have to be endowed with uncommon qualities in the present world. The first things we would have to take into account are his/her culture, political philosophy, religious beliefs, service vocation, commitment to a cause which is above, not only his/her personal interests, whatever they may be, but even those of his/her own country; such a person would have to act in an objective and impersonal fashion, in accordance with the position and not with himself/herself.

Given these personal and status circumstances, some believe that it would have been more practical to constitute an international Court for Human Rights, patterned after that of The Hague, but only for human rights; but perhaps this would make the process become more arduous, difficult and delayed, given the urgency that there presently is in the world for the enforcement, guarantee and exercise of human rights. Nevertheless, there are very effective precedents, with a recognized juridical, moral and ethical solvency, such as the Inter-American Commission on Human Rights (Spanish acronym CIDH) in the Inter-American System, and the Human Rights Court headquartered in Costs Rica, albeit the jurisdictional scope of these is limited to the Western Hemisphere. This does not detract any value from the effectiveness of their work in over three decades that the CIDH has existed, for instance, and the precedents and juridical institutions that it has been able to bring forth, above all in the subject of denouncement (State-person) and the ethical and juridical scope of its conclusions.

2) Will the countries which violate human rights recognize and respect the authority and jurisdiction of the High Commissioner?

We already have an experience with the Rapporteurs, who have been denied entry into countries that violate human rights, as in the case of Castro's totalitarian regime. Allegations for that denial are not valid and excuses are totally unacceptable.

Some violator countries allege that:

A)   Their sovereignty is infringed upon;

B)   It constitutes an interference with the country's internal affairs;

C) National Jurisdiction is infringed upon, since they erroneously believe that it is incumbent upon them to investigate and punish such violations;

D) National boundaries are infringed upon;

E) Human rights violations are internal affairs for each State, and a superior power has no incumbency upon them.

All of these arguments are absolutely false; they have only served and still serve to cover up the monstrous violations of human rights committed and still in force in many countries, such as Cuba, North-Korea, Viet-Nam, Haiti, Maymar (Birmania), Iran, etc., as it has been recently stated by the United Nations. it is not lawful for anybody to deny their universality.

3) The creation of the Legal and Institutional Framework (Protocol) that would be the juridical, ethical and moral foundation for the acts of the High Commissioner.

4) The kinds of denouncements on violations, their subjects and objects:

A) The state affected, whose Citizens' rights have been violated;

B) Citizens of a state against their own Government;

C) Citizens of a state against another State.

5) Violations of Human Rights can be committed in their dual dimension:

A) Institutional Dimension, when contained in the Constitution and laws, in the legal system in force, if we could call it such, whereby the monstrosity is committed to "legally infringe upon" human rights;

B) Human Dimension, committed both by leftist and rightist regimes. In the former, they are abuses of authority by autocratic regimes and, in the latter, they are totalitarian abuses (leftist Marxist-Leninist regimes such as that in Cuba, the last bulwark of communist in this Hemisphere, as they state).

6)   Will investigations "in loco" of the denounced violations be allowed them, or will they be covered up, restricted or the necessary evidence be destroyed? (The UN General Assembly approved on December 20, 1993, by 74 votes, the statement about violations of human rights in Cuba. It's been proved undoubtedly and confessed in writing by Castro himself that he exposed the Cuban people to suffer nuclear extermination only to serve the Soviet Union and the Socialist Marxist-Leninist movement).

When we are dealing with the violation of human rights in its dual dimension: Institutional Violation and Human Violation, as we have demonstrated and proven in this book, it does not matter if the High Commissioner for Human Rights is denied entry into the violator country; it would suffice for him/her to obtain a copy of that country's Constitution, the Penal Code, the Code of Procedures or any other legal instrument officially published, in order to demonstrate and evidence the violation of human rights, as the Inter-American Commission on Human Rights has done with denouncements of the Institutional Violations that we have provided it, and such as the Rapporteur of the United Nations has also done with the Institutional Violations that we have contributed for his information.

The Institutional Violation is undoubted and irrefutable, above all boundaries and sovereignties. This is a proof of the universality of human rights.

Respect, guarantee, enforcement, exercise and compliance with human rights, inalienable and imprescriptible, and obedience for them, comes from a higher authority and law, that transcends human power.

ANNEXES

TEN ORIGINAL AMENDMENTS: THE BILL OF RIGHTS
In force December 15, 1791

Amendment I

Religious establishment prohibited. Freedom of speech, of the press, and right to petition.

Congress shall make no law respecting an establishment of religion, or prohibiting the free exercise thereof;   or abridging the freedom of speech, or of the press;   or the right of the people peaceably to assemble, and to petition the Government for redress of grievances.

Amendment II

Right to keep and bear arms.

A well regulated Militia, being necessary to the security of a free State, the right of the people to keep and bear arms, shall not be infringed.

Amendment III

Conditions for quarters of soldiers.

No soldier shall, in time of peace be quartered in any house without the consent of the owner, nor in time of war, but in a manner to be prescribed by law.

Amendment IV

Rights of search and seizure regulated.

The right of the people to be secure in their persons, houses, papers, and effects against unreasonable searches and seizures, shall not be violated, and no warrants shall issue, but upon probable cause, supported by oath or affirmation, and particularly describing the place to be searched, and the persons or things to be seized.

Amendment V

Provisions concerning prosecution. Trial and punishment, private property not to be taken for public use without compensation.

No person shall be held to answer for a capital, or otherwise infamous crime, unless on a presentment or indictment of a Grand Jury, except in cases arising in the land or naval forces, or in the militia, when in actual service in time of war or public danger; nor shall any person be subject for the same offense to be twice put in jeopardy of life or limb; nor shall be compelled in any criminal case to be a witness against himself, nor be deprived of life, liberty, or property, without due process of law, nor shall private property be taken for public use, without just compensation.

Amendment VI
Right to speedy trial, witnesses, etc.

In all criminal prosecutions, the accused shall enjoy the right to a speedy trial, by an impartial jury of the State and district wherein the crime shall have been committed, which district shall been previously ascertained by law, and to be informed of the nature and cause of the accusation; to be confronted with the witnesses against him; to have compulsory process for obtaining witnesses in his favor and to have the assistance of counsel for his defense.

Amendment VII

Right of trial by jury.

In suits at common law, where the value in controversy shall exceed twenty dollars, the right of trial by jury shall be preserved, and no fact tried by a jury shall be otherwise reexamined in any court of the United States, than according to the rules of the common law.

Amendment VIII

Excessive bail or fines and cruel punishment prohibited.

Excessive bail shall not be required, nor excessive fines imposed, nor cruel and unusual punishments inflicted.

Amendment IX

Rule of construction of Constitution.

The enumeration in the Constitution, of certain rights, shall not be construed to deny or disparage others retained by the people.

Amendment X

Rights of States under Constitution.

The powers not delegated to the United States by the Constitution, nor prohibited by it to the States are reserved to the States respectively, or to the people.

AMERICAN DECLARATION OF THE RIGHTS
AND DUTIES OF MAN

(Adopted by the Ninth International Conference of
American States, Bogota, Colombia, 1948

WHEREAS:

The American peoples have acknowledged the dignity of the individual, and their national constitutions recognize that juridical and political institutions, which regulate life in human society, have as their principal aim the protection of the essential rights of man and the creation of circumstances that will permit him to achieve spiritual and material progress and attain happiness;

The American States have on repeated occasions recognized that the essential rights of man are not derived from the fact that he is a national of a certain state, but are based upon attributes of his human personality;

The international protection of the rights of man should be the principal guide of an evolving American law;

The affirmation of essential human rights by the American States together with the guarantees given by the internal regimes of the states establish the initial system of protection considered by the American States as being suited to the present social and juridical conditions, not without a recognition on their part that they should increasingly strengthen that system in the international field as conditions become more favorable.

The Ninth International Conference of American States

AGREES

To adopt the following:

AMERICAN DECLARATION OF THE RIGHTS AND DUTIES OF MAN

Preamble

All men are born free and equal, in dignity and in rights, and, being endowed by nature with reason and conscience, they should conduct themselves as brothers one to another.

The fulfillment of duty by each individual is a prerequisite to the rights of all. Rights and duties are interrelated in every social and political activity of man. While rights exalt individual liberty, duties express the dignity of that liberty.

Duties of a juridical nature presuppose others of a moral nature which support them in principle and constitute their basis.

Inasmuch as spiritual development is the supreme end of human existence and the highest expression thereof, it is the duty of man to serve that end with all his strength and resources.

Since culture is the highest social and historical expression of that spiritual development, it is the duty of man to preserve, practice and foster culture by every means within his power.

And, since moral conduct constitutes the nobles flowering of culture, it is the duty of every man always to hold it in high respect.

CHAPTER ONE

Rights

Right to life, liberty and personal security.

Article I. Every human being has the right to life, liberty and the security of his person.

Right to equality before the law.

Article II. All persons are equal before the law and have the rights and duties established in this Declaration, without distinction as to race, sex, language, creed or any other factor.

Right to religious freedom and worship.

Article III. Every person has the right freely to profess a religious faith, and to manifest and practice it both in public and in private.

Right to freedom of investigation, opinion, expression and dissemination.

Article IV. Every person has the right to freedom of investigation, of opinion, and of the expression and dissemination of ideas, by any medium whatsoever.

Right to protection of honor, personal reputation and private and family life.

Article V. Every person has the right to the protection of the law and against abusive attacks upon his honor, his reputation, and his private and family life.

Rights to a family and to protection thereof.

Article VI. Every person has the right to establish a family, the basic element of society, and to receive protection therefor.
Right to protection for mothers and children.

Right to protection for mothers and children.

Article VII. All women, during pregnancy and the nursing period, and all children have the right to special protection, care and aid.

Right to residence and movement.

Article VIII.   Every person has the right to fix his residence within the territory of the state of which he is a national, to move about freely within such territory, and not to leave it except by his own will.

Right to inviolability of home.

Article IX.   Every person has the right to the inviolability of his home.

Right to the inviolability and transmission of correspondence.

Article X.   Every person has the right to the inviolability and transmission of his correspondence.

Right to the preservation of health and to well-being.

Article XI.   Every person has the right to the preservation of his health through sanitary and social measures relating to food, clothing, housing and medical care, to the extent permitted by public and community resources.

Right to education.

Article XII.   Every person has the right to an education,   which should be based on the principles of liberty, morality and human solidarity.

Likewise every person has the right to an education that will prepare him to attain a decent life, to raise his standard of living, and to be a useful member of society.

The right to an education includes the right to equality of opportunity in every case, in accordance with natural talents, merit and the desire to utilize the resources that the state or the community is in a position to provide.

Every person has the right to receive, free, at least a primary education.

Right to the benefits of culture.

Article XIII. Every person has the right to take part in the cultural life of the community, to enjoy the arts, and to participate in the benefits that result from intellectual progress, especially scientific discoveries.

He likewise has the right to the protection of his moral and material interests as regards his inventions or any literary, scientific or artistic works of which he is the author.

Right to work and to fair remuneration.

Article XIV. Every person has the right to work, under proper conditions, and to follow his vocation freely, in so far as existing conditions of employment permit.

Every person who works has the right to receive such remuneration as will, in proportion to his capacity and skill, assure him a standard of living suitable for himself and for his family.

Right to leisure time and to the use thereof.

Article XV. Every person has the right to leisure time, to wholesome recreation, and to the opportunity for advantageous use of his free time to his spiritual, cultural and physical benefit.

Right to social security.

Article XVI. Every person has the right to social security which will protect him from the consequences of unemployment, old age, and disabilities arising from causes beyond his control that make it physically or mentally impossible for him to earn a living.

Right to recognition of juridical personality and of civil rights.

Article XVII.   Every person has the right to be recognized everywhere as a person having rights and obligations, and to enjoy the basic civil rights.

Right to a fair trial.

Article XVIII.   Every person may resort to the courts to ensure respect for his legal rights.   There should likewise be available to him a simple,   brief procedure whereby the courts will protect him from acts of authority that,   to his prejudice,   violate any fundamental constitutional rights.

Right to nationality.

Article XIX.   Every person has the right to the nationality to which he is entitled by law and to change it, if he so wishes, for the nationality of any other country that is willing to grant it to him.

Right to vote and to participate in government.

Article XX.   Every person having legal capacity is entitled to participate in the government of his country,   directly or through his representatives,   and to take party in popular elections,   which shall be by secret ballot,   and shall be honest,   periodic and free.

Right of assembly.

Article XXI.   Every person has the right to assemble peaceably with others in a formal public meeting or an informal gathering,   in connection with matters of common interest of any nature.

Right of association.

Article XXII.   Every person has the right to associate with others to promote,   exercise and protect his legitimate interests of a political,   economic,   religious,   social,   cultural,   professional,   labor union or other nature.

Right to property.

Article XXIII. Every person has a right to own such private property as meets the essential needs of decent living and helps to maintain the dignity of the individual and of the home.

Right of petition.

Article XXIV. Every person has the right to submit respectful petitions to any competent authority, for reasons of either general or private interest, and the right to obtain a prompt decision thereon.

Right of protection from arbitrary arrest.

Article XXV. No person may be deprived of his liberty except in the cases and according to the procedures established by pre-existing law.

No person may be deprived of liberty for nonfulfillment of obligations of a purely civil character.

Right to due process of law.

Article XXVI. Every accused person is presumed to be innocent until proved guilty.

Every person accused of an offense has the right to be given an impartial and public hearing, and to be tried by courts previously established in accordance with pre-existing laws, and not to receive cruel, infamous or unusual punishment.

Right of asylum.

Article XXVII. Every person has the right, in case of pursuit not resulting from ordinary crimes, to seek and receive asylum in foreign territory, in accordance with the laws of each country and with international agreements.

Scope of the rights of man.

Article XXVIII. The rights of man are limited by the rights of others, by the security of all, and by the just demands of the general welfare and the advancement of democracy.

CHAPTER TWO

Duties

Duties to society.

Article XXIX. It is the duty of the individual so to conduct himself in relation to others that each and every one may fully form and develop his personality.

Duties toward children and parents.

Article XXX. It is the duty of every person to aid, support, educate and protect his minor children to honor their parents always and to aid, support and protect them when they need it.

Duty to receive instruction.

Article XXXI. It is the duty of every person to acquire at least an elementary education.

Duty to vote.

Article XXXII. It is the duty of every person to vote in the popular elections of the country of which he is national, when he is legally capable of doing so.

Duty to obey the law.

Article XXXIII. It is the duty of every person to obey the law and other legitimate commands of the authorities of his country and those of the country in which he may be.

Duty to serve the community and the nation.

Article XXXIV. It is the duty of every able-bodied person to render whatever civil and military service his country may require for its defense and preservation, and, in case of public disaster, to render such services as may be in his power.

It is likewise his duty to hold any public office to which he may be elected by popular vote in the state of which he is a national.

Duties with respect to social security and welfare.

Article XXXV. It is the duty of every person to cooperate with the state and the community with respect to social security and welfare, in accordance with his ability and with existing circumstances.

Duty to pay taxes.

Article XXXVI. It is the duty of every person to pay the taxes established by law for the support of public services.

Duty to work.

Article XXXVII. It is the duty of every person to work, as far as his capacity and possibilities permit, in order to obtain the means of livelihood or to benefit his community.

Duty to refrain from political activities in a foreign country.

Article XXXVIII. It is the duty of every person to refrain from taking part in political activities that, according to law, are reserved exclusively to the citizens of the state in which he is an alien.

UNIVERSAL DECLARATION
OF
HUMAN RIGHTS

On December 10, 1948, the General Assembly of the United Nations adopted and proclaimed the Universal Declaration of Human Rights, the full text of which appears in the following pages. Following this historic act the Assembly called upon all Member countries to publicize the text of Declaration and "to issue it to be disseminated, displayed, read and expounded principally in schools and other educational institutions with out distinction based on the political status of countries or territories."

Final Authorized Text

UNITED NATIONS

OFFICE OF PUBLIC INFORMATION

UNIVERSAL DECLARATION
OF HUMAN RIGHTS

PREAMBLE

Whereas recognition of the inherent dignity and of the equal and inalienable rights of all members of the human family is the foundation of freedom, justice and peace in the world,

Whereas disregard and contempt for human rights have resulted in barbarous acts which have outraged the conscience of mankind, and the advent of a world in which human beings shall enjoy freedom of speech and belief and freedom from fear and want has been proclaimed as the highest aspiration of the common people,

Whereas it is essential, if man is not to be compelled to have recourse, as a last resort, to rebellion against tyranny and oppression, that human rights should be protected by the rule of law,

Whereas it is essential to promote the development of friendly relations between nations,

Whereas the parties of the United Nations have in the Charter reaffirmed their faith in fundamental human rights, in the dignity and worth of the human person and in the equal rights of men and women and have determined to protect real progress and better standards of life,

Whereas Member States have pledged themselves to achieve in co-operation with the United Nations, the promotion of universal respect for and observance of human rights and fundamental freedom,

Whereas a common understanding of these rights and freedoms is of the greatest importance for the full realization of this pledge,

Now Therefore,

THE GENERAL ASSEMBLY

Proclaims

THIS UNIVERSAL DECLARATION OF HUMAN RIGHTS as a common standard of achievement for all peoples and all nations, to the end that every individual and every organ of society, keeping this Declaration constantly in mind, shall strive by teaching and education to promote respect for these rights and freedoms and by progressive measures, national and international, to secure their universal effective recognition and observance, both among the peoples of Member States themselves and among the peoples of territories under their jurisdiction.

Article 1. All human beings are born free and equal in dignity and rights. They are endowed with reason and conscience and should act towards one another in a spirit of brotherhood.

Article 2. Everyone is entitled with all the rights and freedoms set forth in this Declaration, without distinction of any kind, such as race, color, sex, language, religion, political or other opinion, national or social origin, property, birth or other status.

Furthermore, no distinction shall be made on the basis of the political, jurisdictional or international status of the country or territory to which a person belongs, whether it be independent, trust, non-self-governing or under any other limitation of sovereignty.

Article 3. Everyone has the right to life, liberty and security of person.

Article 4. No one shall be held in slavery or servitude; slavery and the slave trade shall be prohibited in all their forms.

Article 5. No one shall be subjected to torture or to cruel, inhuman or degrading treatment or punishment.

Article 6. Everyone has the right to recognition everywhere as a person before the law.

Article 7. All are equal before the law and are entitled without any discrimination to equal protection under the law. All are entitled to equal protection against any discrimination in violation of this Declaration and against any incitement to such discrimination.

Article 8. Everyone has the right to an effective remedy by the competent national tribunals for acts violating the fundamental rights granted him by the constitution or by law.

Article 9. No one shall be subjected to arbitrary arrest, detention or exile.

Article 10. Everyone is entitled in full equality to a fair and public hearing by an independent and impartial tribunal, in the determination of his rights and obligations and any criminal charges against him.

Article 11. (1) Everyone charged with a penal offense has the right to be presumed innocent until proved guilty according to law in a public trial at which he has had all the guarantees necessary for his defense. (2) No one shall be held guilty of any penal offense on account of any act or omission which did not constitute a penal offense, under national or international law at the time when it was committed. Nor shall a heavier penalty be imposed than the one that was applicable at the time the penal offense was committed.

Article 12. No one shall be subjected to arbitrary interference with his privacy, family, home or correspondence, nor to attacks upon his honor and reputation. Everyone has the right to the protection of the law against such interference or attacks.

Article 13. (1) Everyone has the right to freedom of movement and residence within the borders of each state. (2) Everyone has the right to leave any country, including his own, and to return to his country.

Article 14. (1) Everyone has the right to seek and to enjoy in other countries asylum from persecution. (2) This right may not be invoked in the case of prosecutions genuinely arising from non-political crimes or from acts contrary to the purposes and principles of the United Nations.

Article 15. (1) Everyone has the right to a nationality. (2) No one shall be arbitrarily deprived of his nationality not denied the right to change his nationality.

Article 16. (1) Men and women of full age, without any limitation due to race, nationality or religion, have the right to marry and to found a family. They are entitled to equal rights as to marriage, during marriage and at its dissolution. (2) Marriage shall be entered into only with the free and full consent of the intending spouses. (3) The family is the natural and fundamental group unit of society and is entitled to protection by society and the State.

Article 17. (1) Everyone has the right to own property alone as well as in association with others. (2) No one shall be arbitrarily deprived of his property.

Article 18. Everyone has the right to freedom of thought, conscience and religions; this right includes freedom to change his religion or belief, and freedom, either alone or in community with others and in public or private, to manifest his religion or belief in teaching, practice, worship and observance.

Article 19. Everyone has the right to freedom of opinion and expression; this right includes freedom to hold opinions without interference and to seek, receive and impart information and ideas through any media and regardless of frontiers.

Article 20. (1) Everyone has the right to freedom of peaceful assembly and association. (2) No one may be compelled to belong to an association.

Article 21. (1) Everyone has the right to take part in the government of his country, directly or through freely chosen representatives. (2) Everyone has the right of equal access to public service in his country. (3) The will of the people shall be the basis of the authority of government, this will shall be expressed in periodic and genuine elections which shall be by universal and equal suffrage and shall be held by secret vote or by equivalent free voting procedures.

Article 22. Everyone, as a member of society, has the right to social security and is entitled to realization, through national effort and international co-operation and in accordance with the organization and resources of each State, of the economic, social and cultural rights indispensable for his dignity and the free development of his personality.

Article 23.　　(1) Everyone has the right to work, to free choice of employment, to just and favorable conditions of work and to protection against unemployment. (2) Everyone, without any discrimination, has the right to equal pay for equal work. (3) Everyone who works has the right to just and favorable remuneration ensuring for himself and his family an existence worthy of human dignity, and supplemented, if necessary, by other means of social protection. (4) Everyone has the right to form and to join trade unions for the protection of his interests.

Article 24.　　Everyone has the right to rest and leisure, including reasonable limitation of working hours and periodic holidays with pay.

Article 25.　　(1) Everyone has the right to a standard of living adequate for the health and well-being of himself and of his family, including food, clothing, housing and medical care and necessary social services, and the right to security in the event of unemployment, sickness, disability, widowhood, old age or other lack of livelihood in circumstances beyond his control. (2) Motherhood and childhood are entitled to special care and assistance. All children, whether born in or out of wedlock, shall enjoy the same social protection.

Article 26.　　(1) Everyone has the right to education. Education shall be free, at least in the elementary and fundamental stages. Elementary education shall be compulsory. Technical and professional education shall be made generally available and higher education shall be equally accessible to all on the basis of merit. (2) Education shall be directed to the full development of the human personality and to the strengthening of respect for human rights and fundamental freedoms. It shall promote understanding, tolerance and friendship among all nations, racial or religious groups, and shall further the activities of the United Nations for the maintenance of peace. (3) Parents have a prior right to choose the kind of education that shall be given to their children.

Article 27.　　(1) Everyone has the right freely to participate in the cultural life of the community, to enjoy the arts and to share in scientific advancement and its benefits. (2) Everyone has the right to the protection of the moral and material interests resulting from any scientific, literary or artistic production of which he is the author.

Article 28.   Everyone is entitled to a social and international order in which the rights and freedoms set forth in this Declaration can be fully realized.

Article 29.   (1) Everyone has duties to the community in which alone the free and full development of his personality is possible. (2) In the exercise of his rights and freedoms, everyone shall be subject only to such limitations as are determined by law solely for the purpose of securing due recognition and respect for the rights and freedoms of others and of meeting the just requirements of morality, public order and the general welfare in a democratic society. (3) These rights and freedoms may in no case be exercised contrary to the purposes and principles of the United Nations.

Article 30.   Nothing in this Declaration may be interpreted as implying for any State, group or person any right to engage in any activity or to perform any act aimed at the destruction of any of the rights and freedoms set forth herein.

GENERAL TEXTS

EUROPEAN CONVENTION FOR THE PROTECTION OF THE RIGHTS OF MAN AND OF THE BASIC LIBERTIES[1]

(Roma, November 4, 1950)

The signatory Governments, members of the Council of Europe.

WHEREAS : The Universal Declaration of the Rights of Man, proclaimed by the General Assembly of the United Nations on December 10, 1948;

WHEREAS : This Declaration tends to insure the universal and effective acknowledgment and application of the rights enunciated in it;

WHEREAS : The purpose of the Council of Europe is that of attaining a closer union among its members, and that one of the means to achieve this purpose is the protection and development of the rights of man and of the basic liberties;

Reaffirming its profound attachment to these basic liberties that make up the very foundations of justice and peace in the world, and the maintenance of which essentially rests, on the one part, upon a truly democratic political regime, and on the other, upon a common conception and respect for the rights of man invoked by them;

Determined, in the capacity of Governments of European States, imbued by a same spirit and in the possession of a common patrimony of ideals and political traditions of respect for freedom and preeminence of Law, to adopt the first adequate measures to insure the collective guarantee for a certain number of rights enunciated in the Universal Declaration;

They have agreed the following:

---

[1] Version taken from Truyol Serra, Antonio, "Los Derechos Humanos", Editorial Tecnos, Madrid, Spain, 1968.

Article 1.- The High Contracting Parties recognize to every person depending upon their jurisdictions, the rights and liberties defined on Title I of this Convention.

TITLE 1

Article 2.-1. The right of every person to life is protected by the Law. Death cannot be intentionally afflicted upon anyone, except for the execution of a capital punishment sentence pronounced by a court, in the case that the felony will be punished through this penalty by the Law.

2.   Death shall not be deemed as inflicted with violation of this article when it is brought about because of a resort to force that is absolutely necessary:

>   a)   To insure the defense of any person against illegal violence;

>   b)   To perform a legal detention or to prevent the flight of a legally detained person;

>   c)   To quell, in accordance with the law, a revolt or an insurrection.

Article 3.- No person can be subjected to torture nor to inhuman or degrading penalties or treatments.

Article 4. - 1. No person can be kept in slavery or servitude.

2.   No person can be forced to perform forced or compulsory work.

3.   In the sense of this article, the following shall not be deemed as "forced or compulsory work":

>   a)   All work normally required of a person subjected to a penalty of imprisonment in the circumstances contemplated by Article 5 of this Convention, or during his/her parole;

>   b)   All service of a military nature or, in the case of conscientious objectors in those countries where conscientious

objection is recognized as legitimate, any other service that will replace compulsory military service;

     c)   All service required when any emergency or calamity shall threaten life or the well-being of the community;

     d)   All work or service that is a part of normal civic duties.

Article 5.- 1. Every person is entitled to freedom and security. Nobody can be deprived of his/her freedom, except in the following cases and in accordance with the procedure established by law:

     a)   If he/she is legally detained or is serving a sentence given by a competent court;

     b)   If he/she has been legally incarcerated or detained, because of contempt for an order given in accordance with the law, by a court, or to guarantee compliance with an obligation established by law;

     c)   If he/she has been detained and incarcerated with the purpose of having him/her appear before the competent judicial authority, when there will be a reasonable suspicion that an infraction has been committed, or when there are reasonable motives to believe in the necessity of preventing him/her to commit an infraction, or to flee after having committed it;

     d)   If the case pertains to the legal detention of a minor, performed with the purpose of educating him/her under surveillance, or his/her legal detention with the purpose of taking him/her before the competent authority;

     e)   If the case is the legal detention of a person likely to propagate a contagious disease, or of a mentally deranged person, an alcoholic, a narcotics addict or a vagrant;

     f)   If the case is the arrest or legal detention of a person in order to prevent him/her to illegally enter the territory, or against whom there are underway proceedings for expulsion or extradition.

2.   Every detained person must be informed, in the shortest term and in a language he/she understands, about the reasons for his/her detention and any accusation made against him/her.

3.   Every person detained or incarcerated in the circumstances detailed on paragraph 1.c) of this article, must be immediately taken before a judge or other magistrate qualified by law to exercise functions, and he/she has the right to be tried within a reasonable period of time, or released during the proceedings. The release can be conditioned to a guarantee that shall insure the attendance of the interested party to the trial.

4.   Every person deprived of his/her freedom through arrest or detention is entitled to submit a recourse before a court, in order for the latter to rule in a short period of time about the equality of his/her detention and to order his/her release if the detention is illegal.

5.   Every person who is the victim of an arrest or a detention in circumstances contrary to the provisions of this article, is entitled to a reparation.

Article 6.- 1. Every person has the right to have his/her trial to be heard fairly and publicly in a reasonable period of time, by an independent and impartial court established by law, which shall decide either upon his/her civil rights and duties, or upon the foundation of any criminal accusation directed against him/her. The sentence must be made public, but access to the hearing room can be prohibited to the press and the public during the entirety or a part of the proceedings, for the interest of morality, of the public order or of national security in a democratic society, when the interests of minors or the protection of the private lives of the parties in the proceedings shall require, or in the measure deemed by the court as strictly necessary, when in special circumstances publicity could be harmful for the interests of justice.

2.   Every person charged with an infraction is presumed innocent until his/her guilt shall have been legally established.

3.   Every accused person has, as a minimum, the following rights:

    a)   To be informed, in the shortest possible period of time, in a language that he/she understands and in a detailed manner, about the nature and reason of the charge directed against him/her;

b)   To have the necessary time and facilities for the preparation of his/her defense;

c)   To defend himself/herself or to have the assistance of a defender of his/her election and, should the person lack the means to pay his/her defender, to be assisted free of charge by a court-appointed lawyer, when the interests of justice shall so require;

d)   To question the accusation witnesses, or to have them questioned, and to obtain the summoning and the questioning of the defense witnesses in the same circumstances as the accusation witnesses;

e)   To obtain free assistance by an interpreter, should the accused person not understand or speak the language utilized in the proceedings.

Article 7.- 1. No person can be convicted for an action or an omission that, when it was committed, did not constitute an infraction according to national or international law. Likewise, a lengthier sentence than that in force at the time the infraction was committed, cannot be imposed.

2.   This article shall not invalidate the sentence or penalty imposed upon a person convicted of an action or of an omission which, at the time it was committed, constituted a crime in accordance with the general principles of law recognized by civilized nations.

Article 8.- 1. Every person is entitled to respect for his/her private and family life, his/her residence and his/her correspondence.

2.   There cannot be any interference by public authority in the exercise of this right, except for the measure in which this interference shall be contemplated by law and shall constitute a measure that, in a democratic society, shall be necessary for national security, public security, the economic well-being of the country, the defense of order and the prevention of criminal infractions, the protection of health or morals, or the protection of the rights and liberties of others.

Article 9.- 1. Every person is entitled to freedom of thought, of conscience and of religion; this right implies the freedom to change religion or conviction, as well as the freedom to express his/her religion or conviction individually or collectively, in public or in private, through the worship, teaching, practices and compliance with rites.

2.   Freedom to express religion or convictions cannot be the subject of more restrictions that those which, foreseen by law, constitute necessary measures in a democratic society for public security, the protection of order, health or public morals, or the protection of the rights and liberties of others.

Article 10.- 1. Every person is entitled to freedom of expression. This right comprises freedom of opinion and the liberty to receive or to communicate information or ideas without the interference of public authorities and regardless of frontiers. This article does not prevent the States from subjecting radio-broadcasting, cinematographic or television enterprises to a regime of prior authorization.

2.   The exercise of these liberties, since it implies duties and responsibilities, may be subjected to certain formalities, conditions, restrictions or sanctions contemplated by law, which shall constitute necessary measures in a democratic society for national security, territorial integrity or public safety, the defense of order and the prevention of crime, protection of health or morals, the protection of the prestige or rights of another to prevent the dissemination of confidential information or to guarantee the authority and impartiality of the judiciary power.

Article 11.- 1. Every person is entitled to the freedom of peaceful assembly and to the freedom of association, including the right to establish with others, labor unions and to join labor unions for the defense of their interests.

2.   The exercise of these rights cannot be subject to any other restrictions than those which, foreseen by law, constitute necessary measures, in a democratic society, for national security, public safety, defense of order and prevention of crime, protection of health or morals, or protection of the rights and liberties of others. This article does not forbid the imposition of legitimate restrictions to the exercise of these rights for members of the armed forces, the police or the Administration of the State.

Article 12.- From the nubile age, men and women have the right to marry and to establish a family according to the national laws that rule the exercise of this right.

Article 13.- Any person whose rights and freedoms, recognized in this Convention, have been violated, has the right to be granted an effective appeal before a national court of first instance, including the case when the violation has been committed by persons acting in the exercise of their official functions.

Article 14.- The enjoyment of the rights and freedoms recognized in this Convention must be assured without any distinction, such as those based on sex, race, color, language, religion, political opinions or any other whatsoever, national or social origin, membership in a national minority, wealth, birth or any other circumstance.

Article 15.- 1. In case of war or any other public danger that threatens the life of the nation, any High Contracting Party can adopt measures to repeal the obligations contemplated in this Convention, in the strict manner required by the situation, and provided that such dispositions are not opposed to the other obligations proceeding from international law.

2. The preceding provision does not authorize any repeal of Article 2nd., except for the case of deaths resulting from legal war actions, nor of Articles 3rd., 4th. (clause 1) and 7th.

3. Any High Contracting Party that will exercise this right of repeal shall keep fully informed the Secretary General of the European Council about the measures taken and the reasons that have prompted them. It shall likewise inform the Secretary General of the European Council about the date on which those measures will have ceased to be in force and when the provisions of the Convention will again have a full application.

Article 16.- None of the provisions in Articles 10, 11 and 14 can be construed as directed to forbid the High Contracting Parties from establishing restrictions to the political activities of foreigners.

Article 17.- None of the provisions of this Convention can be interpreted in the sense that it implies for a State, group or individual, any right to engage in an activity or to perform an act directed to the destruction of the rights or freedoms recognized in this Convention, nor wider limitations of these rights or freedoms than those contemplated in said Convention.

Article 18.- Those restrictions which, in the terms of this Convention, will be established to the aforesaid rights and freedoms, cannot be applied except with the purpose for which they have been contemplated.

TITLE II

Article 19.- With the purpose to insure respect for the obligations resulting from this Convention for the High Contracting Parties, the following are instituted:

> a) An European Commission for the Rights of Man, henceforth called "the Commission".

> b) An European Court for the Rights of Man, henceforth called "The Court".

TITLE III

Article 20.- The Commission is made up by a number of members equivalent to that of the High Contracting Parties. The Commission cannot include more than one member from the same State.

Article 21.- 1. The members of the Commission are elected by the Committee of Ministers, by an absolute majority of votes, from a list of names prepared by the Board of the Consultative Assembly; each group of representatives of the High Contracting Parties in the Consultative Assembly shall submit three candidates among which two, at least, shall be of their same nationality.

2. In the measure that it could be applicable, the same procedure shall be followed to complete the Commission, in the case that other States shall subsequently become Parts in this Convention and to fill the positions that may become vacant.

Article 22.- 1. The members of the Commission are elected for a period lasting six years. They are re-eligible. However, regarding the members designated in the first election, the functions of seven of them shall end in a period of three years.

2.	The members whose terms are to finish at the end of the initial period of three years, shall be designated by lottery performed by the Secretary General of the European Council, immediately after the first election has taken place.

3.	The member of the Commission elected to replace another member whose mandate has not expired, shall cease in his/her functions upon the expiration of his/her predecessor's mandate.

4.	The members of the Commission shall continue in their functions until they are replaced. After this replacement, they shall constitute to process the matters already entrusted them.

Article 23.- Members of the Commission are parts of the same on an individual basis.

Article 24.- Any Contracting Party may denounce to the Commission, through the Secretary General of the European Council, any violation of the provisions of this Convention that it believes may be imputed to another Contracting Party.

Article 25.- **1.** The Commission may know any complaint addressed to the Secretary General of the European Council by any physical person, non-governmental organization or group of private parties, who will deem themselves to be the victims of a violation by one of the High Contracting Parties, of the rights acknowledged in this Convention, in the case where the High Contracting Party has declared to recognize the competence of the Commission in this matter. The High Contracting Parties that have underwritten such a declaration oblige themselves to not placing any obstacle to the exercise of this right.

2.	These declarations can be made for a specific period.

3.	They shall be transmitted to the Secretary General of the European Council, who shall transmit copies to the High Contracting Parties and shall take care of their publication.

4. The Commission shall not exercise the competence attributed to it by this article until at least six High Contracting Parties shall be linked by the declaration foreseen in the preceding paragraphs.

Article 26.- The Commission cannot be required until after the discussion of internal recourse, such as it is understood in accordance with the generally recognized principles of international law and within the term of six months counted from the date of the definitive internal decision.

Article 27.- 1. The Commission shall not take into account any claim submitted for the application of Article 25, when:

a)   It is anonymous;

b)   It is essentially the same as a claim previously determined by the Commission, or which has been submitted to any other international instance for inquiry or settlement, and it does not contain new facts.

2. The Commission shall deem inadmissible any complaint submitted for the application of Article 25, when it shall consider it as incompatible with the provisions of this Convention, or evidently ill-founded, or abusive.

3. The Commission shall reject any complaint that it considers as inadmissible because of the application of Article 26.

Article 28.- In case the Commission accepts the complaint;

a)   With the purpose of determining the facts, it shall conduct a contradictory examination of the complaint with the representatives of the parties and, should it be pertinent, an inquiry, for the efficient implementation of which the interested States shall provide all necessary conveniences, after an exchange of opinions with the Commission;

b)   It shall place itself to the disposal of the interested parties with the purpose of attaining a friendly settlement of the matter, inspired upon respect for the rights of man, as recognized by this Convention.

Article 29.- 1. The Commission shall accomplish the functions contemplated in Article 26 through a sub-commission made up by seven members of the Commission.

2.　　　　Each interested party may designate a member of its choice to be part of the sub-commission.

3.　　　　The remaining members shall be designated by lottery, in accordance with the provisions established by the internal regulations of the Commission.

Article 30.- Should the Commission achieve a friendly settlement, in accordance with Article 28, the sub-commission shall redact a report that shall be transmitted to the interested States, to the Committee of Ministers and to the Secretary General of European Council, with the purpose of publishing it. This report shall be limited to a brief statement of the facts and of the adopted solution.

Article 31.- 1. If a solution has not been attained, the Commission shall redact a report in which it shall explain the facts and shall formulate an opinion about whether the verified facts constitute, on the part of the interested State, a violation of the obligations incumbent upon it in accordance with the Convention. The opinions of all members of the Commission about this matter may be included in said report.

2.　　　　The report shall be conveyed to the Committee of Ministers; it shall likewise be communicated to the interested States, which shall not have any authority to publish it.

3.　　　　Upon transmitting the report to the Committee of Ministers, the Commission may formulate those proposals that it may deem adequate.

Article 32.- 1. If in a period of three months, counting from the date of transmission of the Commission's report to the Committee of Ministers, the matter has not been conveyed to the Court because of the application of Article 48 of this Convention, the Committee of Ministers shall decide, by a majority vote of two thirds of the representatives entitled to be parts of it, whether or not there has been a violation of the provisions of the Convention.

2.　　　　In an affirmative case, the Committee of Ministers shall set the term in which the interested High Contracting Party must adopt the measures derived from the decision of the Committee of Ministers.

3.   If the interested High Contracting Party has not taken any satisfactory measures within the term granted, the Committee of Ministers, through the majority established in paragraph 1 of this article, shall determine which consequences derive from its initial decision, and shall publish the report.

4.   The High Contracting Parties oblige themselves to consider as mandatory for them any decision that the Committee of Ministers may adopt by virtue of the preceding paragraphs.

Article 33.- The Commission assembles behind closed doors.

Article 34.- The decisions of the Commission shall be taken by a majority of members present and voting; the decisions of the sub-commission shall be taken by a majority of its members.

Article 35.- The Commission shall assemble when circumstances warrant it. It shall be called by the Secretary General of the European Council.

Article 36.- The Commission shall redact its internal regulations.

Article 37.- The secretary of the Commission shall remain assured by the Secretary General of the European Council.

TITLE IV

Article 38.- The European Court for the Rights of Man is made up by a number of judges equivalent to that of the members of the European Council. There shall be no two judges who are nationals of the same State.

Article 39.- **1.** The members of the Court are elected by the Consultative Assembly by a majority of the votes cast, from a list of persons submitted by the members of the European Council, and each of the latter shall submit three candidates, from whom at least two must be their nationals.

2.   To the extent possible, the same procedure shall be followed to complete the Court in case new members shall join the European Council and to cover those positions that shall become open.

3.   Candidates must enjoy the highest moral reputation and shall meet the requirements demanded for the exercise of high judiciary functions, or must be legal experts with a recognized competency.

Article 40.- 1. Members of the Court are chosen for a period of nine years. They are re-eligible. However, regarding members designated in the first election, the terms of four of them shall expire at the end of three years, and those of another four shall expire at the end of six years.

2.   Those members whose terms shall expire in the initial periods of three and six years, shall be designated through a lottery performed by the Secretary General of the European Council, immediately after having performed the first election.

3.   The member of the Court chosen to replace another member whose term has not expired, shall cease in his/her functions upon the termination of the term of mandate or his/her predecessor.

4.   Members of the Court shall remain in their posts until being replaced. After this replacement, they shall continue to process those matters that had already been entrusted them.

Article 41.- The Court shall elect its president and its vice-president for a period of three years. These are re-eligible.

Article 42.- Members of the Court shall receive allowances that shall be set by the Committee of Ministers.

Article 43.- For the consideration of each matter place before the Court, the latter shall assemble in a court made up by seven judges. It shall be formed, in an official character, by the judge of the nationality of each interested State or, lacking this, a person chosen by lottery upon the initiative of the President, before starting to consider the case.

Article 44.- Only the High Contracting Parties and the Commission are empowered to resort to the Court.

Article 45.- The competence of the Court extends to all matters regarding the interpretation and application of this Convention, that the High Contracting Parties or the Commission shall submit to it, under the circumstances foreseen in Article 48.

Article 46.- 1. Each of the High Contracting Parties may, at any time, declare that it recognizes as mandatory, in full right and without any special covenant, the jurisdiction of the Court for all matters regarding the interpretation and application of this Convention.

2. The declarations referred to in the preceding paragraph could be made purely and simply, or with condition of reciprocity on the part of several or certain other High Contracting Parties, or for a specified term.

3. These declarations shall be conveyed to the Secretary General of the European Council, who shall transmit copies of them to the High Contracting Parties.

Article 47.- A matter can only be submitted to the Court after the Commission has verified the failure of the friendly settlement and within the term of three months foreseen in Article 32.

Article 48.- On condition that the High Contracting Party interested, if there is but one, or of the High Contracting Parties interested, if there are more than one, shall be subjected to the mandatory jurisdiction of the Court or, in its default, with the consent or agreement of the High Contracting Party interested, if there is but one, or of the High Contracting Parties interested, if there are more than one, the Court can be required:

a)   By the Commission;

b)   By a High Contracting Party, when the victim will be one of its nationals;

c)   By a High Contracting Party which has submitted the case to the Commission;

d)   By a High Contracting Party which has been challenged.

Article 49.- In the case that the Court's competency is challenged, the Court shall decide.

Article 50.- If the ruling of the Court states that a decision taken or a measure ordered by a judicial authority or any other authority of a Contracting party is entirely or partly in opposition to obligations derived from this Convention, and if the internal law of said Party only allows to erase the consequences of said decision or measure in an imperfect manner, the ruling of the Court shall allow, if it is pertinent, an equitable satisfaction to the aggrieved part.

Article 51.- 1. The ruling of the Court shall be motivated.

2. If the sentence does not state, entirely or in part, the unanimous opinion of the judges, any judge shall have the right to attach to same the manifestation of his/her individual opinion.

Article 52.- The ruling of the Court shall be definitive.

Article 53.- The High Contracting Parties oblige themselves to conform with the rulings of the Court in those lawsuits where they are parties.

Article 54.- The ruling of the Court shall be transmitted to the Committee of Ministers, which body shall watch its enforcement.

Article 55.- The Court shall prepare its regulations and shall set its proceedings.

Article 56.- 1. The first election for members of the Court shall take place after the declarations from the High Contracting Parties to which Article 46 refers will have reached the number of eight.

2. The Court shall not be susceptible of being required before this election.

TITLE V

Article 57.- Any High Contracting Party shall provide, upon request from the Secretary General of the European Council, the pertinent explanations about the manner in which its internal Law assures the effective application of any provisions in this Convention.

Article 58.- The expenses of the Commission and of the Court shall be in charge of the European Council.

Article 59.- The members of the Commission and of the Court enjoy, during the performance of their functions, the privileges and immunities foreseen in

Article 40 of the Statutes for the European Council and in the agreements completed by virtue of this Article.

Article 60.- Neither of the provisions of this Convention shall be interpreted in the sense of restricting or hampering those rights of man and fundamental liberties that could be recognized in accordance with the laws of any High Contracting party or of any other Covenant in which it is a party.

Article 61.- Neither of the provisions of this Convention affects the powers conferred to the Committee of Ministers by the Statutes of the European Council.

Article 62.- The High Contracting Parties waive reciprocally, excepting a special commitment, to avail themselves of the treaties, covenants or declarations existing between them, in order to submit, by the way of a complaint, a difference arisen from the interpretation or the application of this Convention, to a procedure for solution different than those foreseen in this Convention.

Article 63.- **1.** Any State can, at the time of ratification or at any other ulterior time, declare in a notification addressed to the Secretary General of the European Council, that this Convention shall apply to all territories or to any one of the territories whose international relations it assures.

2. The Convention shall apply to the territory or territories designated in the notification, starting on the thirtieth day following the date on which it received the notification from the Secretary General of the European Council.

3. In the above mentioned territories, the provisions of this Convention shall be applicable taking into account the local necessities.

4. Each State that has made a declaration of conformity with the first paragraph of this article can, at any subsequent time, declare that it accepts the competency of the Commission regarding one or several of the territories in question, to receive the complaints of physical persons, of nongovernmental organizations or of groups of private parties, in accordance with Article 25 of this Convention.

Article 64.- **1.** Any state can, at the time of the signature of this Convention or the deposit of an instrument for ratification, state a reservation regarding a particular provision of the Convention, to the extent that a law then in force in its territory will be in conflict with this provision. This article does not authorize reservations of a general nature.

2. Any reservation made in accordance with this article, shall be accompanied by a brief description of the law that it refers to.

Article 65.- 1. A High Contracting Party can only denounce this Convention at the end of a term of five years, starting on the date when the Convention was effective for that Party, and through a prior notice of six months given in a notification addressed to the Secretary General of the European Council, who shall inform the other Contracting Parties.

2. This denouncement cannot have as its purpose to separate the interested High Contracting Party from the obligations contained in this Convention in what regards any event that, being able to constitute a violation of these obligations, shall have been effected by said Party prior to the date on which the denouncement takes effect.

3. Under the same reservation, any High Contracting Party which ceases to be a member of the European Council, shall cease being a part to this Convention.

4. The Convention can be denounced in accordance with provisions in the preceding paragraphs, regarding any territories in which it would have been declared as applicable under the terms of Article 63.

Article 66.- 1. This Convention is open for the signatures of the Members of the European Council. It shall be ratified. The ratification's shall be deposited with the Secretary General of the European Council.

2. This Convention shall be effective after the deposit of ten instruments for ratification.

3. For all signatories who ratify it subsequently, the Convention shall be effective from the moment when the instrument for ratification is verified as deposited.

4. The Secretary General of the European Council shall notify all members of the European Council about the effectiveness of the Convention, the names of the High Contracting Parties which have ratified it, as well as

the deposits of all instruments for ratification that shall have taken place subsequently.

Made in Rome on November 4, 1950, in French and English, which texts are due equal faith, in a single copy that shall be deposited in the archives of the European Council. The Secretary General shall transmit certified copies to all signatories.

ADDITIONAL PROTOCOLS[2]
ADDITIONAL PROTOCOL TO THE CONVENTION FOR THE PROTECTION
OF THE RIGHTS OF MAN AND THE BASIC FREEDOMS

The signatory Governments, members of the European Council,

Determined to take adequate measures to assure the collective guarantee of rights and freedoms other than those already present on Title I of the Convention for the Protection of the Rights of Man and the Basic Freedoms, signed in Rome on November 4, 1950 (henceforth called "the Convention"),

Have agreed upon the following:

Article 1.- Any physical or moral person is entitled to respect for his/her properties. No person can be deprived of his/her property except by reason of public usefulness and in the circumstances foreseen by law and the general principles of International Law.

The preceding provisions are understood notwithstanding the right possessed by the States to enact those laws they may deem necessary to regulate the use of properties, in accordance with general interest or to insure the payment of taxes or other contributions, or of fines.

Article 2.- No person can be denied the right to instruction. The State, in the exercise of those functions that it shall assume in the filed of instruction and teaching, shall respect the right of parents to insure this instruction and this teaching in accordance with their religious and philosophical convictions.

---

[2]   Version taken from Truyol Serra, Antonio, "Los Derechos Humanos" (The Human Rights), Editorial Tecnos, Madrid, Spain, 1968.

Article 3.- The High Contracting Parties oblige themselves to organize, at reasonable intervals, free elections with secret scrutinies, in circumstances that assure the free expression of the popular opinion about the election of the legislative body.

Article 4.- Any High Contracting Party can, at the time of the signature or of the ratification of this Protocol, or at any subsequent time, notify the Secretary General of the European Council a declaration indicating to what extent it obliges itself to apply the provisions of this Protocol to such or which territories as designated on said declaration and for which it assures international relationships.

Every High Contracting Party that will have notified a declaration by virtue of the preceding paragraph, can from time to time notify a new declaration modifying the terms of any previous declaration or terminating the application of this Protocol in any territory.

A declaration made in accordance with this article shall be considered as having been made in accordance with paragraph 1 in Article 63 of the Convention.

Article 5.- The High Contracting Parties consider Articles 1, 2, 3 and 4 of this Protocol as additional articles to the Convention and all the provisions of the Convention shall be applied consequently.

Article 6.- This Protocol is open for the signatures of Members of the European Council, signatories to the Convention; it shall be ratified at the same time as the Convention or after the ratification of the latter. It shall take effect after the deposit of ten instruments for ratification. For any signatory who shall ratify it subsequently, the Protocol shall be in force from the moment when the deposit of the instrument for ratification is verified.

The instrument for ratification shall be deposited with the Secretary General of the European Council, who shall notify all Members the names of those who will have ratified it.

Made in Paris on March 20, 1952, in French and English, both texts being due equal faith, in a single copy that shall be deposited in the archives of the European Council. The Secretary General shall transmit a certified copy to each of the signatory Governments.

Annex E

DECLARATION OF THE RIGHTS OF THE CHILD

[Proclaimed by the General Assembly of the United Nations on November 20, 1959 (Resolution 1386 - XIV)]

PREAMBLE

Whereas: The peoples of the United Nations have reaffirmed in its Charter their faith in the fundamental rights of man, and in the dignity and value of the human person, and their determination to promote social progress and raise the level of living within a wider concept of freedom.

Whereas: The United Nations have proclaimed in the Universal Declaration of Human Rights that every person has all rights and freedoms enunciated in same, with no distinction whatsoever because of race, color, sex, language, religion, political opinion or of any other kind, national or social origin, financial position, birth or any other circumstance.

Whereas: The child, because of his/her lack of physical and mental maturity, needs special protection and care, including due legal protection, both before and after his/her birth.

Whereas: The necessity for that special protection has been enunciated in the Geneva Declaration of 1924 on the Rights of the Child, and recognized in the universal Declaration of Human Rights and in those covenants that constitute the specialized organisms and international organizations concerned with the welfare of children.

Whereas: Humankind owes the child the best that can be given him/her,

The General Assembly

Proclaims the present Declaration of the Rights of the Child, in order that he/she may have a happy childhood and enjoy, for his/her own well-being and the well-being of society, those rights and freedoms that are enunciated in it, and it urges parents, men and women individually, and private organizations, local authorities and national governments to recognize those rights and struggle for the observance of same with legislative and other kinds of measures, progressively enacted in accordance with the following principles:

Principle 1

The child shall enjoy all rights enunciated in this Declaration. These rights shall be recognized for all children, with no exception, distinction or discrimination by reasons of race, color, sex, language, religion, political opinions or of any other kind, national or social origin, financial position, birth or any other circumstance, be they of the child himself/herself or of his/her family.

Principle 2

The child shall enjoy a special protection and shall be availed of opportunities and services, all of them provided by law and other means, in order for him/her to be able to develop physically, mentally, morally, spiritually and socially in a healthy and normal manner, as well as within circumstances of freedom and dignity. Upon enacting laws for this purpose, the basic consideration that shall be kept in mind shall be the superior interest of the child.

Principle 3

The child has the right, upon his/her birth, to a name and a nationality.

Principle 4

The child must enjoy the benefits of social security. He/she shall have the right to grow and develop in good health: for this purpose, special care must be provided both to him/her and to his/her mother, including prenatal and postnatal care. The child shall have the right to enjoy adequate feeding, shelter, recreation and medical services.

Principle 5

The physically or mentally-handicapped child, or the child who suffers because of any social impediment, must receive the special treatment, education and care required by his/her particular case.

Principle 6

The child, for the full and harmonious development of his/her personality, needs love and understanding. Whenever it will be possible, he/she must grow under the Protection and responsibility of his/her parents and, at any rate, in an environment of affection and moral and material security; except for extraordinary circumstances, the very young child must not be separated from his/her mother. Society and public authorities shall have the duty of caring especially for children who have no relatives or who lack adequate means of sustenance For the maintenance of children members of large families, it is advisable to grant state subsidies or of any other kind.

Principle 7

The child is entitled to receive education, which shall be free and mandatory at least in the elementary stages. He/she shall be given an education that shall enhance his/her general culture and allow him/her, in circumstances of equality for opportunities, to develop his/her aptitudes and individual criterion, his/her sense of moral and social responsibility, and to become a useful member of society.

The child's superior interest must be the guiding principle for those who have responsibility for his/her education and orientation; said duty is incumbent, in the first instance, upon his/her parents.

The child must fully enjoy games and recreational activities, which must be oriented towards the ends sought by education; society and public authorities shall strive to promote the enjoyment of this right.

Principle 8

The child must, in all circumstances, appear among the first to receive protection and relief.

Principle 9

The child must be Protected against all forms of desertion, cruelty and exploitation He/she shall not be the object of any kind of trade.

The child shall not be allowed to work before an adequate minimum age: in no case shall he/she engage in, nor shall he/she be allowed to engage, in any kind of occupation or employment that may damage his/her health or education, or otherwise prevent his/her physical, mental or moral development.

Principle 10

The child must be protected against those practices that may foster racial, religious or any other kind of discrimination. He/she must be educated in a spirit of understanding, tolerance, friendship among peoples, peace and universal fraternity, and with a full consciousness that he/she must devote his/her energies and aptitudes to the service of his/her fellow beings.

Annex F

AMERICAN CONVENTION ON HUMAN RIGHTS

PREAMBLE

The American states signatory to the present Convention,

Reaffirming their intention to consolidate in this hemisphere, within the framework of democratic institutions, a system of personal liberty and social justice based on respect for the essential rights of man;

Recognizing that the essential rights of man are not derived from one's being a national of certain state, but are based upon attributes of the human personality and that they therefore justify international protection in the form of a convention reinforcing or complementing the protection provided by the domestic law of the American States;

Considering that these principles have been set forth in the Charter of the Organization of American States, in the American Declaration of the Rights and Duties of Man, and in the Universal Declaration of Human Rights, and that they have been reaffirmed and defined in other international instruments, worldwide as well as a regional in scope;

Reiterating that, in accordance with the Universal Declaration of Human Rights, the ideal of free men enjoying freedom from fear and want can be achieved only if conditions are created whereby everyone may enjoy his economic, social, and cultural rights, as well as his civil and political rights; and

Considering that the Third Special Inter-American Conference (Buenos Aires, Argentina 1967) approved the incorporation into the Charter of the Organization of broader standards with respect to economic, social, and educational rights and resolved that an Inter-American convention on human rights should determine the structure, competence, and procedure of the organs responsible for these matters,

Have agreed upon the following:

PART I

STATE OBLIGATIONS AND RIGHTS PROTECTED

CHAPTER I

GENERAL OBLIGATIONS

Article 1. Obligation to Respect Rights

1.   The States Parties to this Convention undertake to respect the rights and freedoms recognized herein and to ensure to all persons subject to their jurisdiction the free and full exercise of those rights and freedoms, without any discrimination for reasons of race, color, sex, language, status, birth, or any other social condition.

2.   For the purposes of this Convention, "person" means every human being.

Article 2. Domestic Legal Effects

Where the exercise of any of the rights or freedoms referred to in Article 1 is not already ensured by legislative or other provisions, the States Parties undertake to adopt, in accordance with their constitutional processes and the provisions of this Convention, such legislative or other measures as may be necessary to give effect to those rights or freedoms.

CHAPTER II

CIVIL AND POLITICAL RIGHTS

Article 3. Right to Juridical Personality

Every person has the right to recognition as a person before the law.

Article 4. Right to Life

1.   Every person has the right to have his life respected. This right shall be protected by law and, in general, from the moment of conception. No one shall be arbitrarily deprived of his life.

2.   In countries that have not abolished the death penalty, it may be imposed only for the most serious crimes and pursuant to a final judgment rendered by a competent court and in accordance with a law establishing such punishment, enacted prior to the commission of the crime. The application of such punishment shall not be extended to crimes to which it does not presently apply.

3.   The death penalty shall not be reestablished in states that have abolished it.

4.   In no case shall capital punishment be inflicted for political offenses or related common crimes.

5.   Capital punishment shall not be imposed upon persons who, at the time crime was committed, were under 18 years of age or over 70 years of age; nor shall it be applied to pregnant women.

6.   Every person condemned to death shall have the right to apply for amnesty, pardon, or commutation of sentence, which may be granted in all cases. Capital punishment shall not be imposed while such a petition is pending decision by the competent authority.

Article 5. Right to Human Treatment

1.   Every person has the right to have his physical, mental and moral integrity respected.   .

2.   No one shall be subjected to torture or to cruel, inhuman or degrading punishment or treatment. All persons deprived of their liberty shall be treated with respect for the inherent dignity of the human person.

3.   Punishment shall not be extended to any person other than the criminal.

4.   Accused persons shall, save in exceptional circumstances, be segregated from convicted persons, and shall be subject to separate treatment appropriate to their status as unconvicted persons.

5.   Minors while subject to criminal proceedings shall be separated from adults and brought before specialized tribunals, as speedily as possible, so that they may be treated in accordance with their status as minors.

6.   Punishments consisting of deprivation of liberty shall have as an essential aim the reform and social readaptation of the prisoners.

Article 6. Freedom from Slavery

1.   No one shall be subject to slavery or to involuntary servitude, which are prohibited in all their forms, as are the slave trade and traffic in women.

2.   No one shall be required to perform forced or compulsory labor. This provision shall not be interpreted to mean that, in those countries in which the penalty established for certain crimes is deprivation of liberty at forced labor, the carrying out of such a sentence imposed by a competent court is prohibited. Forced labor shall not adversely affect the dignity or the physical or intellectual capacity of the prisoner.

3.   For the purposes of this article, the following do not constitute forced or compulsory labor:

    a.   work or service normally required of a person imprisoned in execution of a sentence or formal decision passed by the competent judicial authority. Such work or service shall be carried out under the supervision and control of public authorities, and any persons performing such work or service shall not be placed at the disposal of any private party, company, or juridical person;

    b.   military service and, in countries in which conscientious objectors are recognized, national service that the law may provide for in lieu of military service;

c.   service exacted in time of danger or calamity that threatens the existence or the well-being of the community; or

d.   work or service that forms part of normal civic obligations.

Article 7. Right to Personal Liberty

1.   Every person has the right to personal liberty and security.

2.   No one shall be deprived of his physical liberty except for the reasons and under the conditions established beforehand by the constitution of the State Party concerned or by a law established pursuant thereto.

3.   No one shall be subject to arbitrary arrest or imprisonment.

4.   Anyone who is detained shall be informed of the reasons for his detention and shall be promptly notified of the charge or charges against him.

5.   Any person detained shall be brought promptly before a judge or other officer authorized by law to exercise judicial power and shall be brought to trial within a reasonable time, or to released without prejudice to the continuation of the proceedings. His release may be subject to guarantees to assure his appearance for trial.

6.   Anyone who is deprived of his liberty shall be entitled to recourse to a competent court, in order that the court may decide without delay on the lawfulness of his arrest or detention, and order his release if the arrest or detention is unlawful. In States Parties the laws of which provide that anyone who believes himself to be threatened with deprivation of his liberty has the right of recourse to a competent tribunal in order that it may decide on the legality of such threat, this remedy may not be restricted or abolished. The interested party, or another person on his behalf, is entitled to invoke these remedies.

7.   No one shall be detained for debt. This principle shall not limit the orders of a competent judicial authority issued for nonfulfillment of duties of support.

Article 8. Right to a Fair Trial

1. Every person has the right to be heard, with due process guarantees and within a reasonable time, by a competent, independent, and impartial judge or tribunal, previously established by law, in the substantiation or any accusation of a criminal nature made against him or for the determination of his rights and obligations of a civil, labor, fiscal, or any other nature.

2. Every person accused of a criminal offense has the right to be presumed innocent until such time as his guilt has been proven according to law. During the proceedings, every person is entitled, with full equality, to the following minimum guarantees:

   a. the right of the accused to be assisted without charge by a translator or interpreter, if he does not understand or does not speak the language of the tribunal or court;

   b. prior notification in detail to the accused of the charges against him;

   c. adequate time and means for the preparation of his defense;

   d. the right of the accused to defend himself personally or to be assisted by legal counsel of his own choosing, and to communicate freely and privately with his counsel;

   e. the inalienable right to be assisted by counsel provided by the state, paid or not as the domestic law provides, if the accused does not defend himself personally or engage his own counsel within the time period established by law;

   f. the right of the defense to examine witnesses present in the court and to obtain the appearance, as witnesses, of experts or other persons who may throw light on the facts;

g.   the right not to be compelled to testify against himself or to confess guilt; and

h.   the right to appeal the judgment to a higher judge or tribunal.

3.   A confession of guilty by the accused shall be valid only if it is made without coercion of any kind.

4.   An accused person acquitted by a final judgment shall not be subjected to a new trial for the same facts.

5.   Criminal proceedings shall be public, except insofar as may be necessary to protect the interests of justice.

Article 9. Freedom from Ex Post Facto Laws

No one shall be convicted for any act or omission that did not constitute a criminal offense, under the applicable law, at the time it was committed. Nor shall a heavier penalty be imposed than the one that was applicable at the time the criminal offense was committed. If subsequent to the commission of the offense the law provides for the imposition of a lighter punishment, the guilty person shall benefit therefrom.

Article 10. Right to Compensation

Every person has the right to be compensated in accordance with the law in the event that he has been sentenced by a final resulting from a miscarriage of justice.

Article 11. Right to Privacy

1.   Everyone has the right to have one's honor respected and one's dignity recognized.

2.   No one may be the object of arbitrary or abusive interference with respect to one's private life, family, home, or correspondence, or of unlawful attacks on one's honor or reputation.

3.   Everyone has the right to the protection of the law against such interferences or attacks.

Article 12. Freedom of Conscience and Religion

1.   Everyone has the right to freedom of conscience, and religion. This right includes freedom to maintain or to change one's religion or beliefs, either individually or together with others, in public or in private.

2.   No one shall be subject to restrictions that might impair the freedom to maintain or to change one's religion or beliefs.

3.   Freedom to manifest one's religion and beliefs may be subject only to the limitations prescribed by law that are necessary to protect public safety, order, health, or morals, or the rights or freedoms of others.

4.   Parents or guardians, as the case may be, have the right to provide for the religious and moral education of their children or wards that is in accord with their own convictions.

Article 13. Freedom of Thought and Expression

1.   Everyone has the right to freedom of thought and expression. This right includes freedom to seek, receive, and disseminate information and ideas of all kinds, regardless of frontiers, either orally, in writing, in print, in the form of art, or through any other medium of one's choice.

2.   The exercise of the right provided for in the foregoing paragraph shall not be subject to prior censorship but shall be subject to subsequent imposition of liability, which shall be expressly established by law to the extent necessary to ensure:

      a.   respect for the rights or reputation of others; or

      b.   the protection of national security, public order, or public health or morals.

3.   The right of expression may not be restricted by indirect methods or means, such as the abuse of government or private controls over newsprint, radio broadcasting frequencies, or equipment used in the

dissemination of information, or by any other means tending to impede the communication and circulation of ideas and opinions.

4.   Notwithstanding the provisions of paragraph 2 above, public entertainment may be subject by law to prior censorship for the sole purpose of regulating access to them for the moral protection of childhood and adolescence.

5.   Any propaganda for war and any advocacy of national, racial, or religious hatred that constitutes an incitement to lawless violence or to any other similar illegal action against any person or group of persons, on any grounds, including those of race, color, religion, language, or national origin shall be considered as an offense punishable by law.

Article 14. Right of Rectification or Reply

1.   Anyone injured by inaccurate or offensive statements or ideas, disseminated to the public in general, by a legally regulated medium of communication has the right to reply or to a rectification by the same communications outlet, under such conditions as the law may establish.

2.   The rectification or reply shall not excuse other legal liabilities that may have been incurred.

3.   For the effective protection of honor and reputation, every publication or newspaper, motion picture, radio, and television company, shall be represented by a person who is not protected by immunities or special privileges.

Article 15. Right of Assembly

The right of peaceful assembly, without arms, is recognized. No restrictions may be placed on the exercise of this right other than those imposed in conformity with the law and necessary in a democratic society in the interest of national security, public safety or public order, or to protect public health or morals or the rights or freedoms of others.

Article 16. Freedom of Association

1.   Everyone has the right to associate freely for ideological, religious, political, economic, labor, social, cultural, sports or other purposes.

2.   The exercise of this right shall be subject only to such restrictions established by law as may be necessary in a democratic society, in the interest of national security, public safety or public order, or to protect public health or morals or the rights and freedoms of others.

3.   The provisions of this article do not bar the imposition of legal restrictions, including even deprivation of the exercise of the right of association, on members of the armed forces and the police.

Article 17. Rights of the Family

1.   The family is the natural and fundamental group unit of society and is entitled to protection by society and the state.

2.   The right of men and women of marriageable age to marry and to raise a family shall be recognized, if they meet the conditions required by domestic laws, insofar as such conditions do not affect the principle of nondiscrimination established in this Convention.

3.   No marriage shall be entered into without the free and full consent of the intending spouses.

4.   The States Parties shall take appropriate steps to ensure the equality of rights and the adequate balancing of responsibilities of the spouses as to marriage, during marriage, and in the event of its dissolution. In case of dissolution, provision shall be made for the necessary protection of any children solely on the basis of their own best interests.

5. The law shall recognize the equal rights of children born out of wedlock and born in wedlock.

Article 18. Right to Name

Every person has the right to a given name and to the surnames of his parents or to that of one of them. The law shall regulate the manner in which this right shall be ensured for all, by the use of assumed names if necessary.

Article 19. Rights of the Child

Every minor child has the right to the protection required by his condition as a minor from family, society and the state.

Article 20. Right to Nationality

1. Every person has the right to a nationality.

2. Every person has the right to the nationality of the state in which territory he was born if he does not have the right to any other nationality.

3. No one shall be arbitrarily deprived of his nationality or of the right to change it.

Article 21. Right to Property

1. Everyone has the right to the use and enjoyment of his property. The law may subordinate such use and enjoyment to the interest of society.

2. No one shall be deprived of his property except upon payment of just compensation, for reasons of public utility or social interest, and in the cases and according to the forms established by law.

3. Usury and any other form of exploitation of may by man shall be prohibited by law.

Article 22. Freedom of Movement and Residence

1.   Every person lawfully in the territory of a State Party has the right to move about in it, and to reside in it subject to the provisions of the law.

2.   Every person has the right to leave any country freely, including his own.

3.   The exercise of the foregoing rights may be restricted only pursuant to a law, to the extent necessary in a democratic society, to prevent crime or to protect national security, public safety, public order, public morals, public health, or the rights or freedom of others.

4.   The exercise of the rights recognized in paragraph 1 may also be restricted by law in designated zones for reasons of public interest.

5.   No one can be expelled from the territory of the state of which he is a national or be deprived of the right to enter it.

6.   An alien lawfully in the territory of a State Party to this Convention may be expelled from it only pursuant to a decision reached in accordance with law.

7.   Every person has the right to seek and be granted asylum in a foreign territory, in the event he is being pursued for political offenses or related common crimes, in accordance with the legislation of each state and international conventions.

8.   In no case may an alien be deported or returned to a country, regardless of whether or not it is his country of origin, if in that country his right to life or personal freedom is in danger of being violated because of his race, nationality, religion, social status, or political opinions.

9.   The collective expulsion of aliens is prohibited.

Article 23. Right to Participate in Government

1.   Every citizen shall enjoy the following rights and opportunities:

a.	to take part in the conduct of public affairs, directly or through freely chosen representatives;

b.	to vote and to be elected in genuine periodic elections, which shall be by universal and equal suffrage and by secret ballot that guarantees the free expression of the will of the voters; and

c.	to have access, under general conditions of equality, to the public service of his country.

2.	The law may regulate the exercise of the rights and opportunities referred to in the preceding paragraph only on the basis of age, nationality, residence, language, education, civil and mental capacity, or sentencing by a competent court in criminal proceedings.

Article 24. Right to Equal Protection

All persons are equal before the law. Consequently, they are entitled, without discrimination, to equal protection of the law.

Article 25. Right to Judicial Protection

1.	Everyone has the right to a simple and prompt recourse, or any other effective recourse, before a competent court or tribunal for protection against acts that violate one's fundamental rights recognized by the constitution or laws of the state concerned or by this Convention, even though such violation may have been committed by persons acting in the course of their official duties.

2.	The States Parties undertake:

a.	to ensure that any person claiming such remedy shall have his rights determined by the competent authority provided for by the legal system of the state;

b.	to develop the possibilities of judicial remedy; and

c.   to ensure that the competent authorities shall enforce such remedies when granted.

CHAPTER III

ECONOMIC, SOCIAL, AND CULTURAL RIGHTS

Article 26. Progressive Development

The States Parties undertake to adopt measures, both internally and through international cooperation, especially those of an economic and technical nature, with a view to achieving progressively, by legislation or other appropriate means, the full realization of the rights implicit in the economic, social, educational, scientific, and cultural standards set forth in the Charter of the Organization of American States as amended by the Protocol of Buenos Aires.

CHAPTER IV

SUSPENSION OF GUARANTEES, INTERPRETATION AND APPLICATION

Article 27. Suspension of Guarantees

1.   In time of war, public danger, or other emergency that threatens the independence or security of a State Party, it may take measures derogating from its obligations under the present Convention to the extent and for the period of time strictly required by the exigencies of the situation, provided that such measures are not inconsistent with its other obligations under international law and do not involve discrimination on the ground of race, color, sex, language, religion, or social origin.

2.   The foregoing provision does not authorize any suspension of the following articles: Article 3 (Right to Juridical Personality), Article 4 (Right to Life), Article 5 (Right to Human Treatment), Article 6 (Freedom from Slavery), Article 9 (Freedom from Ex Post Facto Laws), Article 12 (Freedom of Conscience and Religion), Article 17 (Rights of the Family), Article 18 (Right to a Name), Article 19 (Right of the Child), Article 20

(Right to Nationality), and Article 23 (Right to Participate in Government), or of the judicial guarantees essential for the protection of such rights.

3. Any State Party availing itself of the right of suspension shall immediately inform the other States Parties, through the Secretary General of the Organization of American States, of the provisions the application of which it has suspended, the reasons that gave rise to the suspension, and the date set for the termination of such suspension.

Article 28. Federal Clause

1. Where a State Party is constituted as a federal state, the national government of such State Party shall implement all the provisions of the Convention over which subject matter it exercises legislative and judicial jurisdiction.

2. With respect to the provisions over which subject matter the constituent units of the federal state have jurisdiction, the national government shall immediately take suitable measures, in accordance with its constitution and its laws, to the end that the competent authorities of the constituent units may adopt appropriate provisions for the fulfillment of this Convention.

3. Whenever two or more States Parties agree to form a federation or other type of association, they shall take care that the resulting compact contains the provisions necessary for continuing and rendering effective the standards of the Convention in the new state that is organized.

Article 29. Restrictions Regarding Interpretation

No provision of this Convention shall be interpreted as:

a. permitting any State Party, group, or person to suppress the enjoyment or exercise of the rights and freedoms recognized in this Convention or to restrict them to a greater extent than is provided for herein;

b. restricting the enjoyment or exercise of any right or freedom recognized by virtue of the laws of any State Party or by virtue of another convention to which one of the said states is a party;

c.   precluding other rights or guarantees that are inherent in the human personality or derived from representative democracy as a form of government; or

d.   excluding or limiting the effect that the American Declaration of the Rights and Duties of Man and other international acts of the same nature may have.

Article 30. Scope of Restrictions

The restrictions that, pursuant to this Convention, may be placed on the enjoyment of exercise of the rights or freedoms recognized herein may not be applied except <u>in accordance with laws enacted for reasons of general interest and</u> in accordance with the purpose for which such restrictions have been established.

Article 31. Recognition of Other Rights

Other rights and freedoms recognized in accordance with the procedures established in Articles 76 and 77 may be included in the system of protection of this Convention.

CHAPTER V

RESPONSIBILITIES

Article 32. Relationship between Duties and Rights

1.   Every person has responsibilities to his family, his community, and mankind.

2.   The rights of each person are limited by the rights of others, by the security of all, and by the just demands of the general welfare, in a democratic society.

PART II

MEANS OF PROTECTION

CHAPTER VI

COMPETENT ORGANS

Article 33

The following organs shall have competence with respect to matters relating to the fulfillment of the commitments made by the States Parties to this Convention:

a.   the Inter-American Commission on Human Rights, referred to as "The Commission"; and

b.   the Inter-American Court of Human Rights, referred to as "The Court".

CHAPTER VII

INTER-AMERICAN COMMISSION ON HUMAN RIGHTS

Section 1. Organization

Article 34

The Inter-American Commission on Human Rights shall be composed of seven members, who shall be persons of high moral character and recognized competence in the field of human rights.

Article 35

The Commission shall represent all the member countries of the Organization of American States.

Article 36

1.   The members of the Commission shall be elected in a personal capacity by the General Assembly of the Organization from a list of candidates proposed by the governments of the member states.

2.   Each of those governments may propose up to three candidates, who may be nationals of the states proposing them or of any other member state of the Organization of American States. When a slate of three is proposed, at least one of the candidates shall be a national of a state other than the one proposing the slate.

Article 37

1.   The members of the Commission shall be elected for a term of four years and may be reelected only once, but the terms of three of the members chosen in the first election shall expire at the end of two years. Immediately following that election the General Assembly shall determine the names of those three members by lot.

2.   No two nationals of the same state may be members of the Commission.

Article 38

Vacancies that may occur on the Commission for reasons other than the normal expiration of term shall be filled by the Permanent Council of the Organization in accordance with the provisions of the Statute of the Commission.

Article 39

The Commission shall prepare its Statute, which it shall submit to the General Assembly for approval. It shall establish its own Regulations.

Article 40

Secretariat services for the Commission shall be furnished by the appropriate specialized unit of the General Secretariat of the Organization. This unit shall be provided with the resources required to accomplish the tasks assigned to it by the Commission.

Section 2. Functions

Article 41

The main function of the Commission shall be to promote respect for and defense of human rights. In the exercise of its mandate, it shall have the following functions and powers:

a. to develop an awareness of human rights among the peoples of the Americas;

b. to make recommendations to the governments of the member states, when it considers such action advisable, for the adoption of progressive measures in favor of human rights within the framework of their domestic law and constitutional provision as well as appropriate measures to further the observance of those rights;

c. to prepare such studies or reports as it considers advisable in the performance of its duties;

d. to request the governments of the member states to supply it with information on the measures adopted by them in matters of human rights;

e. to respond, through the General Secretariat of the Organization of American States, to inquiries made by the member states on matters related to human rights and, within the limits of its possibilities, to provide those states with the advisory services they request;

f. to take action on petitions and other communications pursuant to its authority under the provisions of Article 44 through 51 of this Convention; and

g.   to submit an annual report to the General Assembly of the Organization of American States.

Article 42

The States Parties shall transmit to the Commission a copy of each of the reports and studies that they submit annually to the Executive Committees of the Inter-American Economic and Social Council and the Inter-American Council for Education, Science, and Culture, in their respective fields, so that the Commission may watch over the promotion of the rights implicit in the economic, social, educational, scientific, and cultural standards set forth in the Charter of the Organization of American States as amended by the Protocol of Buenos Aires.

Article 43

The States Parties undertake to provide the Commission with such information as it may request of them as to the manner in which their domestic law ensures the effective application of any provisions of this Convention.

Section 3. Competence

Article 44

Any person or group of persons, or any nongovernmental entity legally recognized in one or more member states of the Organization, may lodge petitions with the Commission containing denunciations or complaints of violations of this Convention by a State Party.

Article 45

1.   Any State Party may, when it deposits its instrument of ratification or adherence to this Convention, or at any later time, declare that it recognizes the competence of the Commission to receive and examine communications in which a State Party alleges that another State Party has committed a violation of human right set forth in this Convention.

2.   Communications presented by virtue of this article may be admitted and examined only if they are presented by a State party that has made a declaration recognizing the aforementioned competence of the Commission. The Commission shall not admit any communication against a State Party that has not made such a declaration.

3.   A declaration concerning recognition of competence may be made to be valid for an indefinite time, for a specified period, or for a specific case.

4.   Declaration shall be deposited with the General Secretariat of the Organization of American States, which shall transmit copies thereof to the member states of that Organization.

Article 46

Admission by the Commission of a petition or communication lodged in accordance with Articles 44 or 45 shall be subject to the following requirements:

a.   that the remedies under domestic law have been pursued and exhausted in accordance with generally recognized principles of internal law;

b.   that the petition or communication is lodged within a period of six months from the date on which the party alleging violation of his rights was notified of the final judgment;

c.   that the subject of the petition or communication is not pending in another international proceeding for settlement; and

d.   that, in the case of Article 44, the petition contains the name, nationality, profession, domicile, and signature of the person or persons of the legal representative of the entity lodging the petition.

2.   The provisions of paragraphs 1.a and 1.b of this article shall not be applicable when:

a. the domestic legislation of the state concerned does not afford due process of law for the protection of the right or rights that have allegedly been violated;

b. the party alleging violation of his rights has been denied access to the remedies under domestic law or has been prevented from exhausting them; or

c. there has been unwarranted delay in rendering a final judgment under the aforementioned remedies.

Article 47

The Commission shall consider inadmissible any petition or communication submitted under Articles 44 or 45 if:

a. any of the requirements indicated in Article 46 has not been met;

b. the petition or communication does not state facts that tend to establish a violation of the rights guaranteed by this Convention;

c. the statements of the petitioner or of the state indicate that the petition or communication is manifestly groundless or obviously out of order; or

d. the petition or communication is substantially the same as one previously studied by the Commission or by another international organization.

Section 4. Procedure

Article 48

1. When the Commission receives a petition or communication alleging violation of any of the rights protected by this Convention, it shall proceed as follows:

    a. if it considers the petition or communication admissible, it shall request information from the government of the state indicated as being responsible for the alleged violations and shall furnish that government a transcript of the pertinent portions of the petition or communication. This information shall be submitted within a reasonable period to be determined by the Commission in accordance with the circumstances of each case;

    b. after the information has been received, or after the period established has elapsed and the information has not been received, the Commission shall ascertain whether the grounds for the petition or communication still exist. If they do not, the Commission shall order the record to be closed;

    c. the Commission may also declare the petition or communication inadmissible or out of order on the basis of information or evidence subsequently received;

    d. if the record has not been closed, the Commission shall, with the knowledge of the parties, examine the matter set forth in the petition or communication in order to verify the facts. If necessary and advisable, the Commission shall carry out an investigation, for the effective conduct of which it shall request, and the states concerned shall furnish to it, all necessary facilities;

    e. the Commission may request the states concerned to furnish any pertinent information and, if so requested, shall hear oral statements or receive written statements from the parties concerned;

g. the Commission shall place itself at the disposal of the parties concerned with a view to reaching a friendly settlement of the matter on the basis of respect for the human rights recognized in this Convention.

2. However, in serious and urgent cases, only the presentation of a petition or communication that fulfills all the formal requirements of admissibility shall be necessary in order for the Commission to conduct an investigation with the prior consent of the state in whose territory a violation has allegedly been committed.

Article 49

If a friendly settlement has been reached in accordance with paragraph 1.f of Article 48, the Commission shall draw up a report which shall be transmitted to the petitioner and to the States Parties to this Convention, and shall then be communicated to the Secretary General of the Organization of American States for publication. This report shall contain a brief statement of the facts and of the solution reached. If any party in the case so requests, the fullest possible information shall be provided to it.

Article 50

1. If a settlement is not reached, the Commission shall, within the time limit established by its Statute, draw up a report setting forth the facts and stating its conclusion. If the report, in whole or in part, does not represent the unanimous agreement of the members of the Commission, any member may attach to it a separate opinion. The written and oral statements made by the parties in accordance with paragraph 1.e of Article 48 shall also be attached to the report.

2. The report shall be transmitted to the state concerned, which shall not be at liberty to publish it.

3. In transmitting the report, the Commission may make such proposals and recommendations as it sees fit.

Article 51

1.   If, within a period of three months from the date of the transmittal of the report of the Commission to the states concerned, the matter has not either been settled or submitted by the Commission or by the state concerned to the Court and its jurisdiction accepted, the Commission may, by the vote of an absolute majority of its members, set forth its opinion and conclusions concerning the question submitted for its consideration.

2.   Where appropriate, the Commission shall make pertinent recommendations and shall prescribe a period within which the state is to take the measures that are incumbent upon it to remedy the situation examined.

3.   When the prescribed period has expired, the Commission shall decide by the vote of an absolute majority of its members whether the state has taken adequate measures and whether to publish its report.

CHAPTER VIII

INTER-AMERICAN COURT OF HUMAN RIGHTS

Section 1. Organization

Article 52

1.   The Court shall consist of seven judges, nationals of the member states of the Organization, elected in an individual capacity from among jurists of the highest moral authority and of recognized competence in the field of human rights, who possess the qualifications required for the exercise of the highest judicial functions in conformity with the law of the state of which they are nationals or of the state that proposes them as candidates.

2.   No two judges may be nationals of the same state.

Article 53

1.   The judges of the Court shall be elected by secret ballot by an absolute majority vote of the States Parties to the Convention, in the General Assembly of the Organization, from a panel of candidates proposed by those states.

2.   Each of the States Parties may propose up to three candidates, nationals of these state that propose them or of any other member state of the Organization of American States. When a slate of three is proposed, at least one of the candidates shall be a national of a state other than the one proposing the slate.

Article 54

1.   The judges of the Court shall be elected for a term of six years and may be reelected only once. The term of three of the judges chosen in the first election shall expire at the end of three years. Immediately after the election, the names of the three judges shall be determined by lot in the General Assembly.

2.   A judge elected to replace a judge whose term has not expired shall complete the term of the latter.

3.   The judges shall continue in office until the expiration of their term. However, they shall continue to serve with regard to cases that they have begun to hear and that are still pending, for which purposes they shall not be replaced by the newly elected judges.

Article 55

1.   If a judge is a national of any of the States Parties to a case submitted to the Court, he shall retain his right to hear that case.

2.   If one of the judges called upon to hear a case should be a national of one of the States Parties to the case, any other State Party in the case may appoint a person of its choice to serve on the Court as an ad hoc judge.

3.   If among the judges called upon to hear a case none is a national of any of the States Parties to the case, each of the latter may appoint an ad hoc judge.

4.   An ad hoc judge shall possess the qualifications indicated in Article 52.

5. If several States Parties to the Convention should have the same interest in a case, they shall be considered as a single party for purposes of the above provisions. In case of doubt, the Court shall decide.

Article 56

Five judges shall constitute a quorum for the transaction of business by the Court.

Article 57

The Commission shall appear in all cases before the Court.

Article 58

1. The Court shall have its seat at the place determined by the States Parties to the Convention in the General Assembly of the Organization; however, it may convene in the territory of any member state of the Organization of American States when a majority of the Court considers it desirable, and with the prior consent of the state concerned. The seat of the Court may be changed by the States Parties to the Convention in the General Assembly by a two-thirds vote.

2. The Court shall appoint its own Secretary.

3. The Secretary shall have its office at the place where the Court has its seat and shall attend the meetings that the Court may hold away from its seat.

Article 59

The Court shall establish its Secretariat, which shall function under the direction of the Secretary of the Court, in accordance with the administrative standards of the General Secretariat of the Organization in all respects not incompatible with the independence of the Court. The staff of the Court's Secretariat shall be appointed by the Secretary General of the Organization, in consultation with the Secretary of the Court.

Article 60

The Court shall draw up its Statute which it shall submit to the General Assembly for approval. It shall adopt its own Rules of Procedure.

Section 2. Jurisdiction and Functions

Article 61

1.   Only the States Parties and the Commission shall have the right to submit a case to the Court.

2.   In order for the Court to hear a case, it is necessary that the procedures set forth in Articles 48 and 50 shall have been completed.

Article 62

1.   A State Party may, upon depositing its instrument of ratification or adherence to this Convention, or at any subsequent time, declare that it recognizes as binding, ipso facto, and not requiring special agreement, the jurisdiction of the Court on all matters relating to the interpretation or application of this Convention.

2.   Such declaration may be made unconditionally, on the condition of reciprocity, for a specified period, or for specific cases. It shall be presented to the Secretary General of the Organization, who shall transmit copies thereof to the other member states of the Organization and to the Secretary of the Court.

3.   The jurisdiction of the Court shall comprise all cases concerning the interpretation and application of the provisions of the Convention that are submitted to it, provided that the States Parties to the case recognize or have recognized such jurisdiction, whether by special declaration pursuant to the preceding paragraphs, or by a special agreement.

Article 63

1.   If the Court finds that there has been a violation of a right or freedom protected by this Convention, the Court shall rule that the injured party be ensured the enjoyment of his right or freedom that was violated. It shall also rule, if appropriate, that the consequences of the measure or situation that constituted the breach of such right or freedom be remedied and that fair compensation be paid to the injured party.

2.   In cases of extreme gravity and urgency, and when necessary to avoid irreparable damage to persons, the Court shall adopt such provisional measures as it deems pertinent in matters it has under consideration. With respect to a case not yet submitted to the Court, it may act at the request of the Commission.

Article 64

1.   The member states of the Organization may consult the Court regarding the interpretation of this Convention or of other treaties concerning the protection of human rights in the American states. Within their spheres of competence, the organs listed in Chapter X of the Charter of the Organization of American States, as amended by the Protocol of Buenos Aires, may in like manner consult the Court.

2.   The Court, at the request of a member state of the Organization, may provide that state with opinions regarding the compatibility of any of its domestic laws with the aforesaid international instruments.

Article 65

To each regular session of the General Assembly of the Organization of American States, the Court shall submit, for the Assembly's consideration, a report on its work during the previous year. It shall specify, in particular, the cases in which a state has not complied with its judgments, making any pertinent recommendations.

Section 3. Procedure

Article 66

1.   Reasons shall be given for the judgment of the Court.

2.   If the judge does not represent in whole or in part the unanimous opinion of the judges, any judge shall be entitled to have his dissenting or separate opinion attached to the judgment.

Article 67

The judgment of the Court shall be final and not subject to appeal. In case of disagreement as to the meaning or scope of the judgment, the Court shall interpret it at the request of any of the parties, provided the request is made within ninety days from the date of notification of the judgment.

Article 68

1.   The States Parties to the Convention undertake to comply with the judgment of the Court in any case to which they are parties.

2.   That part of a judgment that stipulates compensatory damages may be executed in the country concerned in accordance with domestic procedure governing the execution of judgments against the state.

Article 69

The parties to the case shall be notified of the judgment of the Court and it shall be transmitted to the States Parties to the Convention.

CHAPTER X

COMMON PROVISIONS

Article 70

1.   The judges of the Court and the members of the Commission shall enjoy, from the moment of their election and throughout their term of office, the immunities extended to diplomatic agents in accordance with international law. During the exercise of their official function they shall, in addition, enjoy the diplomatic privileges necessary for the performance of their duties.

2.   At no time shall the judges of the Court or the members of the Commission be held liable for any decisions or opinions issued in the exercise of their functions.

Article 71

The position of the judge of the Court or member of the Commission is incompatible with any other activity that might affect the independence or impartiality of such judge or member, as determined in the respective statutes.

Article 72

The judges of the Court and the members of the Commission shall receive emoluments and travel allowances in the form and under the conditions set forth in their statutes, with due regard for the importance and independence of their office. Such emoluments and travel allowances shall be determined in the budget of the Organization of American States, which shall also include the expenses of the Court and its Secretariat. To this end, the Court shall draw up its own budget and submit it for approval to the General Assembly through the General Secretariat. The latter may not introduce any changes in it.

Article 73

The General Assembly may, only at the request of the Commission or the Court, as the case may be, determine sanctions to be applied against members of the Commission or judges of the Court when there are justifiable grounds for such action as set forth in the respective statutes. A vote of a two-thirds majority of the member states of the Organization shall be required for a decision in the case of members of the Commission and, in the case of judges of the Court, a two-thirds majority vote of the States Parties to the Convention shall also be required.

PART III

GENERAL AND TRANSITORY PROVISIONS

CHAPTER X

SIGNATURE, RATIFICATION, RESERVATIONS, AMENDMENTS, PROTOCOLS, AND DENUNCIATION

Article 74

1.   This Convention shall be open for signature and ratification or accession to any member state of the Organization of American States.

2.   Ratification or accession to this Convention shall be effected by the deposit of an instrument of ratification or accession with the General Secretariat of the Organization of American States. As soon as eleven states have deposited their instruments of ratification or accession, the Convention shall enter into force. With respect to any state that ratifies or accedes thereafter, the Convention shall enter into force on the date of the deposit of its instrument of ratification or accession.

3.   The Secretary General shall inform all member states of the Organization of the entry into force of the Convention.

Article 75

This Convention shall be subject to reservations only in conformity with the provisions of the Vienna Convention on the Law of Treaties signed on May 23, 1969.

Article 76

1.   Any State Party may submit, directly, and the Commission or the Court, by means of the Secretary General, any proposed amendment to this Convention to the General Assembly for the action it deems appropriate.

2.   Amendments shall enter into force for the states ratifying them on the date when two-thirds of the States Parties to this Convention have deposited their respective instruments of ratification. With respect to the other States Parties, the amendments shall enter into force on the dates on which they deposit their respective instruments of ratification.

Article 77

1.   In accordance with Article 31, any State Party and the Commission may submit proposed protocols to this Convention for consideration by the States Parties at the General Assembly with a view to gradually including other rights and freedoms within its system of protection.

2.   Each protocol shall determine the manner of its entry into force and shall be applicable only to the States Parties to it.

Article 78

1.   The States Parties may denounce this Convention at the expiration of a five-year period from the date of its entry into force and by means of notice given one year in advance. Notice of the denunciation shall be addressed to the Secretary General of the Organization, who shall inform the other States Parties.

2.   Such a denunciation shall not have the effect of releasing the State Party concerned from the obligations contained in this Convention with respect to any act that may constitute a violation of these obligations incurred by the State prior to the effectiveness of denunciation.

CHAPTER XI

TRANSITORY PROVISIONS

Section 1. Inter-American Commission on Human Rights

Article 79

Upon the entry into force of this Convention, the Secretary General shall, in writing, request each member state of the organization to present, within ninety days, its candidates for membership on the Inter-American Commission on Human Rights. The Secretary General shall prepare a list, in alphabetical order, of the candidates presented and transmit it to the member states of the Organization at least thirty days prior to the next session of the General Assembly.

Article 80

The members of the Commission shall be elected by secret ballot of the General Assembly from the list of candidates referred to in Article 79. The candidates who obtain the largest number of votes and an absolute majority of the votes of the representatives of the member states shall be declared elected. Should it become necessary to have several ballots in order to elect all the members of the Commission, the candidates who receive the smallest number of votes shall be eliminated successively, in the manner determined by the General Assembly.

Section 2. Inter-American Court of Human Rights

Article 81

Upon the entry into force of this Convention, the Secretary General shall, in writing, request each State Party to present, within ninety days, its candidates for membership on the Inter-American Court of Human Rights. The Secretary General shall prepare a list, in alphabetical order, of the candidates presented and transmit it to the States Parties at least thirty days prior to the next session of the General Assembly.

Article 82

The judges of the Court shall be elected from the list of candidates referred to in Article 81, by secret ballot of the States Parties to the Convention in the General Assembly. The candidates who obtain the largest number of votes and an absolute majority of the votes of the representatives of the States Parties shall be declared elected. Should it become necessary to have several ballots in order to elect all the judges of the Court, the candidates who receive the smallest number of votes shall be eliminated successively, in the manner determined by the States Parties.

STATEMENTS AND RESERVATIONS

STATEMENT OF CHILE

The Delegation of Chile signs this Convention, subject to its subsequent parliamentary approval and ratification, in accordance with the constitutional rules in force.

STATEMENT OF ECUADOR

The Delegation of Ecuador has the honor of signing the American Convention on Human Rights. It does not believe that it is necessary to make any specific reservation at this time, without prejudice to the general power set forth in the Convention itself that leaves the governments free to ratify or not.

RESERVATION OR URUGUAY

Article 80.2 of the Constitution of Uruguay provides that citizenship is suspended for a person indicted according to law in a criminal prosecution that may result in a sentence of imprisonment in a penitentiary. This restriction on the exercise of the rights recognized in Article 23 of the Convention is not envisaged among the circumstances provided for in this respect by paragraph 2 of Article 23, for which reason the Delegation of Uruguay expresses a reservation on this matter.

IN WITNESS WHEREOF, the undersigned Plenipotentiaries, whose full powers were found in good and due form, sign this Convention, which shall be called "PACT OF SAN JOSE, COSTA RICA," (in the city of San Jose, Costa Rica, this twenty-second day of November, nineteen hundred and sixty-nine).

DEPARTMENT OF STATE

CONFERENCE ON SECURITY
AND CO-OPERATION IN EUROPE
FINAL ACT

HELSINKI 1975

The Conference on Security and Co-operation in Europe, which opened at Helsinki on 3 July 1973 and continued at Geneva from 18 September 1973 to 21 July 1975, was concluded at Helsinki on 1 August 1975 by the High Representatives of Austria, Belgium, Bulgaria, Canada, Cyprus, Czechoslovakia, Denmark, Finland, France, the German Democratic Republic, the Federal Republic of Germany, Greece, the Holy See, Hungary, Iceland, Ireland, Italy, Liechtenstein, Luxembourg, Malta, Monaco, the Netherlands, Norway, Poland, Portugal, Romania, San Marino, Spain, Sweden, Switzerland, Turkey, the Union of Soviet Socialist Republics, the United Kingdom, the United States of America and Yugoslavia.

During the opening and closing of the Conference the participants were addressed by the Secretary-General of the United Nations as their guest of honor. The Director-General of UNESCO and the Executive Secretary of the United Nations Economic Commission for Europe addressed the Conference during its second stage.

During the meeting of the second stage of the Conference, contributions were received, and statements heard, from the following non-participating Mediterranean States on various agenda items: the Democratic and Popular Republic of Algeria, the Arab Republic of Egypt, Israel, the Kingdom of Morocco, the Syrian Arab Republic, Tunisia.

Motivated by the political will, in the interest of peoples, to improve and intensify their relations and to contribute in Europe to peace, security, justice and co-operation as well as to rapprochement among themselves and with the other States of the world.

Determined, in consequence, to give full effect to the results of the Conference and to assure, among their States and throughout Europe, the benefits deriving from those results and thus to broaden, deepen and make continuing and lasting the process of détente.

The High Representatives of the participating States have solemnly adopted the following:

Questions relating to Security in Europe

The States participating in the Conference on Security and Co-operation in Europe,

Reaffirming their objective of promoting better relations among themselves and ensuring conditions in which their people can live in true and lasting peace free from any threat to or attempt against their security;

Convinced of the need to exert efforts to make détente both a continuing and an increasingly viable and comprehensive process, universal in scope, and that the implementation of the results of the Conference on Security and Co-operation in Europe will be a major contribution to this process;

Considering that solidarity among peoples, as well as the common purpose of the participating States in achieving the aims as set forth by the Conference on Security and Co-operation in Europe, should lead to the development of better and closer relations among them in all fields and thus to overcoming the confrontation stemming from the character of their past relations, and to better mutual understanding;

Mindful of their common history and recognizing that the existence of elements common to their traditions and values can assist them in developing their relations, and desiring to search, fully taking into account the individuality and diversity of their positions and views, for possibilities of joining their efforts with a view to overcoming distrust and increasing confidence, solving the problems that separate them and co-operating in the interest of mankind;

Recognizing the indivisibility of security in Europe as well as their common interest in the development of co-operation throughout Europe and among themselves and expressing their intention to pursue efforts accordingly;

Recognizing the close link between peace and security in Europe and in the world as a whole and conscious of the need for each of them to make its contributions to the strengthening of world peace and security and to the promotion of fundamental rights, economic and social progress and well-being for all peoples;

Have adopted the following:

1.

(a) Declaration on Principles Guiding Relations between Participating States

The participating States,

Reaffirming their commitment to peace, security and justice and the continuing development of friendly relations and co-operation;

Recognizing that this commitment, which reflects the interest and aspirations of peoples, constitutes for each State a present and future responsibility, heightened by experience of the past;

Reaffirming, in conformity with their membership in the United Nations and in accordance with the purposes and principles of the United Nations, their full and active support for the United Nations and for the enhancement of its role and effectiveness in strengthening international peace, security and justice, and in promoting the solution of international problems, as well as the development of friendly relations and co-operation among States;

Expressing their common adherence to the principles which are set forth below and are conformity with the Charter of the United Nations, as well as their common will to act, in the application of these principles, in conformity with the purposes and principles of the Charter of the United Nations;

Declare their determination to respect and put into practice, each of them in its relations with all other participating States, irrespective of their political, economic or social systems as well as of their size, geographical location or level of economic development, the following principles, which all are of primary significance, guiding their mutual relations:

I. *Sovereign equality, respect for the rights inherent in sovereignty*

The participating States will respect each other's sovereign equality and individuality as well as the rights inherent in and encompassed by its sovereignty,   including in particular the right of every State to juridical equality, to territorial integrity and to freedom and political independence. They will also respect each other's right freely to choose and develop its political, social, economic and cultural systems as well as its rights to determine its laws and regulations.

Within the framework of international law, all the participant States have equal rights and duties. They will respect each other's right to define and conduct as it wishes its relations with other States in accordance with international law and in the spirit of the present Declaration. They consider that their frontiers can be changed, in accordance with international law, by peaceful means and by agreement. They also have the right to belong or not to belong to international organizations, to be or not to be a party to bilateral treaties including the right to be or not to be a party to treaties of alliance; they also have the right to neutrality.

II. *Refraining from the threat or use of force*

The participating States will refrain in their mutual relations, as well as in their international relations in general, from the threat or use of force against the territorial integrity or political independence of any State, or in any other manner inconsistent with the purposes of the United Nations and with the present Declaration. No consideration may be invoked to serve to warrant resort to the threat or use of force in contravention of this principle.

Accordingly, the participating States will refrain from any acts constituting a threat of force or direct use of force against another participating State. Likewise they will refrain from any manifestation of force for the purpose of inducing another participating State to renounce the full exercise of its sovereign rights. Likewise they will also refrain in their mutual relations from any act of reprisal by force.

No such threat or use of force will be employed as a means of settling disputes, or questions likely to give rise to disputes, between them.

III. *Inviolability of frontiers*

The participating States regard as inviolable all one another's frontiers as well as the frontiers of all States in Europe and therefore they will refrain now and in the future from assaulting these frontiers.

Accordingly, they will also refrain from any demand for, or act of, seizure and usurpation of part or all of the territory of any participating State.

IV. *Territorial integrity of States*

The participating States will respect the territorial integrity of each of the participating States.

Accordingly, they will refrain from any action inconsistent with the purposes and principles of the Charter of the United Nations against the territorial integrity, political independence or the unity of any participating State, and in particular from any such action constituting a threat or use of force.

The participating States will likewise refrain from making each other's territory the object of military occupation or other direct or indirect measures of force in contravention of international law, or the object of acquisition by means of such measures or the threat of them. No such occupation or acquisition will be recognized as legal.

V. *Peaceful settlements of disputes*

The participating States will settle disputes among them by peaceful means in such a manner as not to endanger international peace and security, and justice.

They will endeavor in good faith and a spirit of co-operation to reach a rapid and equitable solution on the basis of international law.

For this purpose they will use such means as negotiation, inquiry, mediation, conciliation, arbitration, judicial settlement or other peaceful means of their own choice including any settlement procedure agreed to in advance of disputes to which they are parties.

In the even of failure to reach a solution by any of the above peaceful means, the parties to a dispute will continue to seek a mutually agreed way to settle the dispute peacefully.

Participating States, parties to a dispute among them, as well as other participating States, will refrain from any action which might aggravate the situation to such a degree as to endanger the maintenance of international peace and security and thereby make a peaceful settlement of the dispute more difficult.

VI. *Non-intervention in internal affairs*

The participating States will refrain from any intervention, direct or indirect, individual or collective, in the internal or external affairs falling within the domestic jurisdiction of another participating State, regardless of their mutual relations.

They will accordingly refrain from any form of armed intervention or threat of such intervention against another participating State.

They will likewise in all circumstances refrain from any other act of military, or of political, economic or other coercion designed to subordinate to their own interest the exercise by another participating State of the rights inherent in its sovereignty and thus to secure advantages of any kind.

Accordingly, they will, inter alia, refrain from direct or indirect assistance to terrorist activities, or to subversive or other activities directed towards the violent overthrow of the regime of another participating State.

VII. *Respect for human rights and fundamental freedoms, including the freedom of thought, conscience, religion or belief*

The participating States will respect human rights and fundamental freedoms, including the freedom of thought, conscience, religion or belief, for all without distinction as to race, sex, language or religion.

They will promote and encourage the effective exercise of civil, political, economic, social, cultural and other rights and freedoms all of which derive from the inherent dignity of the human person and are essential for his free and full development.

Within this framework the participating States will recognize and respect the freedom of the individual to profess and practice, alone or in community with others, religion or belief acting in accordance with the dictates of his own conscience.

The participating States on whose territory national minorities exist will respect the right of persons belonging to such minorities to equality before the law, will afford them the full opportunity for the actual enjoyment of human rights and fundamental freedoms and will, in this manner, protect their legitimate interests in this sphere.

The participating States recognize the universal significance of human rights and fundamental freedoms, respect for which is an essential factor for the peace, justice and well-being necessary to ensure the development of friendly relations and co-operation among themselves as among all States.

They will constantly respect these rights and freedoms in their mutual relations and will endeavor jointly and separately, including in co-operation with the United Nations, to promote universal and effective respect for them.

They confirm the right of the individual to know and act upon his rights and duties in this field.

In the field of human rights and fundamental freedoms, the participating States will act in conformity with the purposes and principles of the Charter of the United Nations and with the Universal Declaration of Human Rights. They will also fulfill their obligations as set forth in the international declarations and agreements in this field, including inter alia the International Covenants on Human Rights, by which they may be bound.

VII. *Equal rights and self-determination of peoples*

The participating States will respect the equal rights of peoples and their right to self-determination, acting at all times in conformity with the purposes and principles of the Charter of the United Nations and with the relevant norms of international law, including those relating to territorial integrity of States.

By virtue of the principle of equal rights and self-determination of peoples, all peoples always have the right, in full freedom, to determine, when and as they wish, their internal and external political status, without external interference, and to pursue as they wish their political, economic, social and cultural development.

The participating States reaffirm the universal significance of respect for and effective exercise of equal rights and self-determination of peoples for the development of friendly relations among themselves as among all States; they also recall the importance of the elimination of any form of violation of this principle.

IX. *Co-operation among States*

The participating States will develop their co-operation with one another and with all States in all fields in accordance with the purposes and principles of the Charter of the United Nations. In developing the co-operation the participating States will place special emphasis on the fields as set forth within the framework of the Conference on Security and Co-operation in Europe, with each of them making its contribution in conditions of full equality.

They will endeavor, in developing their co-operation as equals, to promote mutual understanding and confidence, friendly and good-neighborly relations among themselves, international peace, security and justice. They will equally endeavor, in developing their co-operation, to improve the well-being of peoples and contribute to the fulfillment of their aspirations through, inter alia, the benefits resulting from increased mutual knowledge and from progress and achievement in the economic, scientific, technological, social, cultural and humanitarian fields. They will take steps to promote conditions favorable to making these benefits available to all; they will take into account the interest of all in the narrowing of differences in the levels of economic development, and in particular the interest of developing countries throughout the world.

They confirm that governments, institutions, organizations and persons have a relevant and positive role to play in contributing toward the achievement of these aims of their co-operation.

They will strive, in increasing their co-operation as set forth above, to develop closer relations among themselves on an improved and more enduring basis for the benefit of peoples.

X. *Fulfillment in good faith of obligations under international law.*

The participating States will fulfill in good faith their obligations under international law, both those obligations arising from the generally recognized principles and rules of international law and those obligations arising from treaties or other agreements, in conformity with international law, to which they are parties.

In exercising their sovereign rights, including the right to determine their laws and regulations, they will conform with their legal obligations under international law; they will furthermore pay due regard to and implement the provisions in the Final Act of the Conference on Security and Co-operation in Europe.

The participating States confirm that in the event of a conflict between the obligations of the members of the United Nations under the Charter of the United Nations and their obligations under the Charter will prevail, in accordance with Article 103 of the Charter of the United Nations.

All the principles set forth above are of primary significance and, accordingly, they will be equally and unreservedly applied, each of them being interpreted taking into account the others.

The participating States express their determination fully to respect and apply these principles, as set forth in the present Declaration, in all aspects, to their mutual relations and co-operation in order to ensure to each participating State the benefits resulting form the respect and application of these principles by all.

The participating States, paying due regard to the principles above and, in particular, to the first sentence of the tenth principle, "Fulfillment in good faith of obligations under international law", note that the present Declaration does not affect their rights and obligations, nor the corresponding treaties and other agreements and arrangements.

The participating States express the conviction that respect for these principles will encourage the development of normal and friendly relations and the progress of co-operation among them in all fields. They also express the conviction that respect for these principles will encourage the development of political contacts among them which in turn would contribute to better mutual understanding of their positions and views.

The participating States declare their intention to conduct their relations with all other States in the spirit of the principles contained in the present Declaration.

(b) Matters related to giving effect to certain of the above Principles

(i) The participating States,

Reaffirming that they will respect and give effect to refraining from the threat or use of force and convinced of the necessity to make it an effective norm of international life,

Declare that they are resolved to respect and carry out, in their relations with one another, inter alia, the following provisions which are in conformity with the Declaration on Principles Guiding Relations between Participating States:

- To give effect and expression, by all the ways and forms which they consider appropriate, to the duty to refrain from the threat or use of force in their relations with one another.

- To refrain from any use of armed forces inconsistent with the purposes and principles of the Charter of the United Nations and the provisions of the Declaration on Principles Guiding Relations between Participating States, against another participating State, in particular from invasion of or attack on its territory.

- To refrain from any manifestation of force for the purpose of inducing another participating State to renounce the full exercise of its sovereign rights.

- To refrain from any act of economic coercion designed to subordinate to their own interest the exercise by another participating State of the rights inherent in its sovereignty and thus to secure advantages of any kind.

- To take effective measures which by their scope and by their nature constitute steps towards the ultimate achievement of general and complete disarmament under strict and effective international control.

- To promote, by all means which each of them consider appropriate, a climate of confidence and respect among peoples consonant with their duty to refrain from propaganda for wars of aggression or for any threat or use of force inconsistent with the purposes of the United Nations and with the Declaration on Principles Guiding Relations between Participating States, against another participating State.

- To make every effort to settle exclusively by peaceful means any dispute between them, the continuance of which is likely to endanger the maintenance of international peace and security in Europe, and to seek, first of all, a solution through the peaceful means set forth in Article 33 of the United Nations Charter.
To refrain from any action which could hinder the peaceful settlement of disputes between the participating States.

(ii) The participating States.

Reaffirming their determination to settle their disputes as set forth in the Principle of Peaceful Settlement of Disputes;

Convinced that the peaceful settlement of disputes is a complement to refraining from threat or use of force, both being essential though not exclusive factors for the maintenance and consolidation of peace and security;

Desiring to reinforce and to improve the methods at their disposal for the peaceful settlement of disputes;

1. Are resolved to pursue the examination and elaboration of a generally acceptable method for the peaceful settlement of disputes aimed at complementing existing methods, and to continue to this end to work upon the "Draft Convention on a European System for the Peaceful Settlement of Disputes" submitted by Switzerland during the second stage of the Conference on Security and Co-operation in Europe, as well as other proposals relating to it and directed towards the elaboration of such a method.

2.	Decide that, on the invitation of Switzerland, a meeting of experts of all the participating States will be convoked in order to fulfill the mandate described in paragraph 1 above within the framework and under the procedures of the follow up to the Conference lad down in the chapter "Follow-up to the Conference".

3.	This meeting of experts will take place after the meeting of the representatives appointed by the Ministers of Foreign Affairs of the participating States, scheduled according to the chapter "Follow-up to the Conference".

2.
Document on confidence-building measures
and certain aspects of security and disarmament

The participating States,

Desirous of eliminating the causes of tension that may exist among them and thus of contributing to the strengthening of peace and security in the world;

Determined to strengthen confidence among them and thus to contribute to increasing stability and security in Europe;

Determined further to refrain in their mutual relations, as well as in their international relations in general, from the threat or use of force against the territorial integrity or political independence of any State, or in any other manner inconsistent with the purposes of the United Nations and with the Declaration on Principles Guiding Relations between Participating States as adopted in this Final Act;

Recognizing the need to contribute to reducing the dangers of armed conflict and of misunderstanding or miscalculation of military activities which could give rise to apprehension, particularly in a situation where the participating States lack clear and timely information about the nature of such activities;

Taking into account considerations relevant to efforts aimed at lessening tension and promoting disarmament;

Recognizing that the exchange of observers by invitation at military maneuvers will help to promote contacts and mutual understanding;

Having studied the question of prior notification of major military movements in the context of confidence-building;

Recognizing that there are other ways in which individual States can contribute further to their common objectives;

Convinced of the political importance of prior notification of major military maneuvers for the promotion of mutual understanding and the strengthening of confidence, stability and security;

Accepting the responsibility of each of them to promote these objectives and to implement this measure, in accordance with the accepted criteria and modalities, as essentials for the realization of these objectives;

Recognizing that this measure deriving from political decision rests upon a voluntary basis;

Have adopted the following:

I

Prior notification of major military maneuvers

They will notify their major military maneuvers to all other participating States through usual diplomatic channels in accordance with the following provisions:

Notification will be given of major military maneuvers exceeding a total of 25,000 troops, independently or combined with any possible air or naval components (in this context the word "troops" includes amphibious and airborne troops). In the case of independent maneuvers of amphibious or airborne troops, or of combined maneuvers involving them, these troops will be included in this total. Furthermore, in the case of combined maneuvers which do not reach the above total but which involve land forces together with significant numbers of either amphibious or airborne troops, or both, notification can also be given.

Notification will be given of major military maneuvers which take place on the territory, in Europe, of any participating State as well as, if applicable, in the adjoining sea area and air space.

In the case of a participating State whose territory extends beyond Europe, prior notification need be given only of maneuvers which take place in an area within 250 kilometers from its frontier facing or shared with any other European participating State, the participating State need not, however, give notification in cases in which that area is also contiguous to the participating State's frontier facing or shared with a non-European non-participating State.

Notification will be given 21 days or more in advance of the start of the maneuvers or in the case of a maneuver arranged at shorter notice at the earliest possible opportunity prior to its starting date.

Notification will contain information of the designation, if any, the general purpose of and the States involved in the maneuver, the type or types and numerical strength of the forces engaged, the area and estimated time-frame of its conduct. The participating States will also, if possible, provide additional relevant information, particularly that related to the components of the forces engaged and the period of involvement of these forces.

Prior notification of other military maneuvers

The participating States recognize that they can contribute further to strengthening confidence and increasing security and stability, and to this end may also notify smaller-scale military maneuvers to other participating States, with special regard for those near the area of such maneuvers.

To the same end, the participating States also recognize that they may notify other military maneuvers conducted by them.

Exchange of observers

The participating States will invite other participating States, voluntarily and on a bilateral basis, in a spirit of reciprocity and goodwill towards all participating States, to send observers to attend military maneuvers.

The inviting State will determine in each case the number of observers, the procedures and conditions of their participation, and give other information which it may consider useful. It will provide appropriate facilities and hospitality.

The invitation will be given as far ahead as is conveniently possible through usual diplomatic channels.

Prior notification of major military movements

In accordance with the Final Recommendations of the Helsinki Consultations the participating States studied the question of prior notification of major military movements as a measure to strengthen confidence.

Accordingly, the participating States recognize that they may, at their own discretion and with a view to contributing to confidence-building, notify their major military movements.

In the same spirit, further consideration will be given by the States participating in the Conference on Security and Co-operation in Europe to the question of prior notification of major military movements, bearing in mind, in particular, the experience gained by the implementation of the measures which are set forth in this document.

Other confidence-building measures

The participating States recognize that there are other means by which their common objectives can be promoted.

In particular, they will, with due regard to reciprocity and with a view to better mutual understanding, promote exchanges by invitation among their military personnel, including visits by military delegations.

* * *

In order to make a fuller contribution to their common objective of confidence-building, the participating States, when conducting their military activities in the area covered by the provisions for the prior notification of major military maneuvers, will duly take into account and respect this objective.

They also recognize that the experience gained by the implementation of the provisions set forth above, together with further efforts, could lead to developing and enlarging measures aimed at strengthening confidence.

II
Questions relating to disarmament

The participating States recognize the interest of all of them in efforts aimed at lessening military confrontation and promoting disarmament which are designed to complement political détente in Europe and to strengthen their security. They are convinced of the necessity to take effective measures in these fields which by their scope and by their nature constitute steps towards the ultimate achievement of general and complete disarmament under strict and effective international control, and which should result in strengthening peace and security throughout the world.

III.
General considerations

Having considered the views expressed on various subjects related to the strengthening of security in Europe through joint efforts aimed at promoting détente and disarmament, the participating States, when engaged in such efforts, will, in this context, proceed, in particular, from the following essential considerations:

- The complementary nature of the political and military aspects of security;

- The interrelation between the security of each participating State and security in Europe as a whole and the relationship which exists, in the broader context of world security, between security in Europe and security in the Mediterranean area;

- Respect for the security interests of all States participating in the Conference on Security and Co-operation in Europe inherent in their sovereign equality;

- The importance that participants in negotiating see to it that information about relevant developments, progress and results is provided on an appropriate basis to other States participating in the Conference on Security and Co-operation in Europe and, in return, the justified interest of any of those States in having their views considered.

Co-operation in the Fields of Economics, of Science and Technology and of the Environment

The participating States,

Convinced that their efforts to develop co-operation in the fields of trade, industry, science and technology, the environment and other areas of economic activity contribute to the reinforcement of peace and security in Europe and in the world as a whole,

Recognizing that co-operation in these fields would promote economic and social progress and the improvement of the conditions of life,

Aware of the diversity of their economic and social systems,

Reaffirming their will to intensify such co-operation between one another, irrespective of their systems.

Recognizing that such co-operation, with due regard for the different levels of economic development, can be developed, on the basis of equality and mutual satisfaction of the partners, and of reciprocity permitting, as a whole, an equitable distribution of advantages and obligations of comparable scale, with respect for bilateral and multilateral agreements.

Taking into account the interests of the developing countries throughout the world, including those among the participating countries as long as they are developing from the economic point of view; reaffirming their will to co-operate for the achievement of the aims and objectives established by the appropriate bodies of the United Nations in the pertinent documents concerning development, it being understood that each participating State maintains the positions it has taken on them; giving special attention to the least developed countries.

Convinced that the growing world-wide economic interdependence calls for increasing common and effective efforts towards the solution of major world economic problems such as food, energy, commodities, monetary and financial problems, and therefore emphasizes the need for promoting stable and equitable international economic relations, thus contributing to the continuous and diversified economic development of all countries.

Having taken into account he work already undertaken by relevant international organizations and wishing to take advantage of the possibilities offered by these organizations, in particular by the United Nations Economic Commission for Europe, for giving effect to the provisions of the final documents of the Conference,

Considering that the guidelines and concrete recommendations contained in the following texts are aimed at promoting further development of their mutual economic relations, and convinced that their co-operation in this field should take place in full respect for the principles guiding relations among participating States as set forth in the relevant document.

Have adopted the following:

1. Commercial Exchanges

General provisions

The participating States,

Conscious of the growing role of international trade as one of the most important factors in economic growth and social progress,

Recognizing that trade represents an essential sector of their co-operation, and bearing in mind that the provisions contained in the above preamble apply in particular to this sector,

Considering that the volume and structure of trade among the participating States do not in all cases correspond to the possibilities created by the current level of their economic, scientific and technological development,

are resolved to promote, on the basis of the modalities of their economic co-operation, the expansion of their mutual trade in goods and services, and to ensure conditions favorable to such development;

recognize the beneficial effects which can result for the development of trade from the application of most favored nation treatment;

will encourage the expansion of trade on as broad a multilateral basis as possible, thereby endeavoring to utilize the various economic and commercial possibilities;

recognize the importance of bilateral and multilateral intergovernmental and other agreements for the long-term development of trade;

note the importance of monetary and financial questions for the development of international trade, and will endeavor to deal with them with a view to contributing to the continuous expansion of trade;

will endeavor to reduce or progressively eliminate all kinds of obstacles to the development of trade;

will foster a steady growth of trade while avoiding as far as possible abrupt fluctuations in their trade:

consider that their trade in various products should be conducted in such a way as not to cause or threaten to cause serious injury - and should the situation arise, market disruption - in domestic markets for these products and in particular to the detriment of domestic producers of like or directly competitive products; as regards the concept of market disruption, it is understood that it should not be invoked in a way inconsistent with the relevant provisions of their international agreements; if they resort to safeguard measures, they will do so in conformity with their commitments in this field arising from international agreements to which they are parties and will take account of the interests of the parties directly concerned;

will give due attention to measures for the promotion of trade and the diversification of its structure;

note that the growth and diversification of trade would contribute to widening the possibilities of choice of products;

consider it appropriate to create favorable conditions for the participation of firms, organizations and enterprises in the development of trade.

Business contacts and facilities

The participating States,

Conscious of the importance of the contribution which an improvement of business contacts, and the accompanying growth of confidence in business relationships, could make to the development of commercial and economic relations,

will take measures further to improve conditions for the expansion of contacts between representatives of official bodies, of the different organizations, enterprises, firms and banks concerned with foreign trade, in particular, where useful, between sellers and users of products and services, for the purposes of studying commercial possibilities, concluding contracts, ensuring their implementation and providing after-sales services;

will encourage organizations, enterprises and firms concerned with foreign trade to take measures to accelerate the conduct of business negotiations;

will further take measures aimed at improving working conditions of representatives of foreign organizations, enterprises, firms and banks concerned with external trade, particularly as follows:

- by providing the necessary information, including information on legislation and procedures relating to the establishment and operation of permanent representation by the above mentioned bodies;

- by examining as favorably as possible requests for the establishment of permanent representation and of offices for this purpose, including, where appropriate, the opening of joint offices by two or more firms;

- by encouraging the provision, on conditions as favorable as possible and equal for all representatives of the above-mentioned bodies, of hotel accommodation, means of communication, and of other facilities normally required by them, as well as of suitable business and residential premises for purposes of permanent representation;

recognize the importance of such measures to encourage greater participation by small and medium sized firms in trade between participating States.

Economic and commercial information

The participating States,

Conscious of the growing role of economic and commercial information in the development of international trade,

Considering that economic information should be of such a nature as to allow adequate market analysis and to permit the preparation of medium and long term forecasts, thus contributing to the establishment of a continuing flow of trade and a better utilization of commercial possibilities,

Expressing their readiness to improve the equality and increase the quantity and supply of economic and relevant administrative information,

Considering that the value of statistical information on the international level depends to a considerable extent on the possibility of its comparability,

will promote the publication and dissemination of economic and commercial information at regular intervals and as quickly as possible, in particular:

- statistics concerning production, national income, budget, consumption and productivity;

- foreign trade statistics drawn up on the basis of comparable classification including breakdown by product with indication of volume and value, as well as country of origin or destination;

- laws and regulations concerning foreign trade;

- information allowing forecasts of development of the economy to assist in trade promotion, for example, information on the general orientation of national economic plans and programs;

- other information to help businessmen in commercial contacts, for example, periodic directories, lists, and where possible, organizational charts of firms and organizations concerned with foreign trade;

will in addition to the above encourage the development of the exchange of economic and commercial information through, where appropriate, joint commissions for economic, scientific and technical co-operation, national and joint chambers of commerce, and other suitable bodies;

will support a study, in the framework of the United Nations Economic Commission for Europe, of the possibilities of creating a multilateral system of notification of laws and regulations concerning foreign trade and changes therein;

will encourage international work on the harmonization of statistical nomenclatures, notable in the United Nations Economic Commission for Europe.

Marketing

The participating States,

Recognizing the importance of adapting production to the requirements of foreign markets in order to ensure the expansion of international trade,

Conscious of the need of exporters to be as fully familiar as possible with and take account of the requirements of potential users,

will encourage organizations, enterprises and firms concerned with foreign trade to develop further the knowledge and techniques required for effective marketing;

will encourage the improvement of conditions for the implementation of measures to promote trade and satisfy the needs of users in respect of imported products, in particular through market research and advertising measures as well as, where useful, the establishment of supply facilities, the furnishing of spare parts, the functioning of after sales services, and the training of the necessary local technical personnel;

will encourage international co-operation in the field of trade promotion, including marketing, and the work undertaken on these subjects within the international bodies, in particular the United Nations Economic Commission for Europe.

2. Industrial co-operation and projects of common interest

Industrial co-operation

The participating States,

Considering that industrial co-operation, being motivated by economic considerations, can

- create lasting ties thus strengthening long-term overall economic co-operation,

- contribute to economic growth as well as to the expansion and diversification of international trade and to a wider utilization of modern technology,

- lead to the mutually advantageous utilization of economic complimentarities through better use of all factors of production, and

- accelerate the industrial development of all those who take part in such co-operation,

propose to encourage the developments of industrial co-operation between the competent organizations, enterprises and firms of their countries;

consider that industrial co-operation may be facilitated by means of intergovernmental and other bilateral and multilateral agreements between the interested parties;

note that in promoting industrial co-operation they should bear in mind the economic structures and the development levels of their countries;

note that industrial co-operation is implemented by means of contracts concluded between competent organizations, enterprises and firms on the basis of economic considerations;

express their willingness to promote measures designed to create favorable conditions for industrial co-operation;

recognize that industrial co-operation covers a number of forms of economic relations going beyond the framework of conventional trade, and that in concluding contracts on industrial co-operation the partners will determine jointly the appropriate forms and conditions of co-operations, taking into account heir mutual interests and capabilities;

recognize further that, if it is in their mutual interest, concrete forms such as the following may be useful for the development of industrial co-operation; joint production of sale, specialization in production and sale, constructions, adaptation and modernization of industrial plants, co-operation for the setting up of complete industrial installations with a view to thus obtaining part of the resultant products, mixed companies, exchanges of «know-how», of technical information, of patents and of licenses, and joint industrial research within the framework of specific co-operation projects;

recognize that new forms of industrial co-operation can be applied with a view to meeting specific needs;

Consider it desirable;

- to improve the quality and the quantity of information relevant to industrial co-operation, in particular the laws and regulations, including those relating to foreign exchange, general orientation of national economic plans and programs as well as program priorities and economic conditions of the market; and

- to disseminate as quickly as possible published documentation thereon;

will encourage all forms of exchange of information and communication of experience relevant to industrial co-operation, including through contacts between potential partners and, where appropriate, through joint commissions for economic, industrial, scientific and technical co-operation, national and joint chambers of commerce, and other suitable bodies;

consider it desirable, with a view to expanding industrial co-operation, to encourage the exploration of co-operation possibilities and the implementation of co-operation projects and will take measures to this end, *inter alia*, by facilitating and increasing all forms of business contacts between competent organizations, enterprises and firms and between their respective qualified personnel;

note that the provisions adopted by the Conference relating to business contacts in the economic and commercial fields also apply to foreign organizations, enterprises and firms engaged in industrial co-operation, taking into account the specific conditions of this co-operation, and will endeavor to ensure, in particular, the existence of appropriate working conditions for personnel engaged in the implementation of co-operation projects;

consider it desirable that proposals for industrial co-operation should be sufficiently specific and should contain the necessary economic and technical data, in particular preliminary estimates of the cost of the project, information on the form of co-operation envisaged, and market possibilities, to enable potential partners to proceed with initial studies and to arrive at decisions in the shortest possible time;

will encourage the parties concerned with industrial co-operation to take measures to accelerate the conduct of negotiations for the conclusion of co-operation contracts;

recommend further the continued examination - for example within the framework of the United Nations Economic Commission for Europe - of means of improving the provision of information to those concerned on general conditions of industrial co-operation and guidance on the preparation of contracts in this field;

consider it desirable to further improve conditions for the implementation of industrial co-operation projects, in particular with respect to:

- the protection of the interests of the partners in industrial co-operation projects, including the legal protection of the various kinds of property involved;

- the consideration, in ways that are compatible with their economic systems, of the needs and possibilities of industrial co-operation within the framework of economic policy and particularly in national economic plans and programs;

consider it desirable that the partners, when concluding industrial co-operation contracts, should devote due attention to provisions concerning the extension of the necessary mutual guidance and the provision of the necessary information during the implementation of these contracts, in particular with a view to attaining the required technical level and quality of the products resulting form such co-operation;

recognize the usefulness of an increased participation of small and medium sized firms in industrial co-operation projects.

Projects of common interest

The participating States,

Considering that their economic potential and their natural resources permit, through common efforts, long-term co-operation in the implementation, including at the regional or sub-regional level, of major projects of common interest, and that these may contribute to the speeding-up of the economic development of the countries participating therein,

Considering it desirable that the competent organizations, enterprises and firms of all countries should be given the possibility of indicating their interest in participating in such projects, and, in case of agreement, of taking part in their implementation,

Noting that the provisions adopted by the Conference relating to industrial co-operation are also applicable to projects of common interest,

regard it as necessary to encourage, where appropriate, the investigation by competent and interested organizations, enterprises and firms of the possibilities for the carrying out of projects of common interest in the fields of energy resources and of the exploitation of raw materials, as well as of transport and communications;

regard it as desirable that organizations, enterprises and firms exploring the possibilities of taking part in projects of common interest exchange with their potential partners, through the appropriate channels, the requisite economic, legal, financial and technical information pertaining to these projects;

consider that the fields of energy interest, in particular, petroleum, natural gas and coal, and the extraction and processing of mineral raw materials, in particular, iron ore and bauxite, are suitable ones for strengthening long-term economic co-operation and for the development of trade with could result;

consider that possibilities for projects of common interest with a view to long-term economic co-operation also exist in the following fields:

-       exchanges of electrical energy within Europe with a view to utilizing the capacity of the electrical power stations as rationally as possible;

-       co-operation in research for new sources of energy and, in particular, in the field of nuclear energy;

-       development of road networks and co-operation aimed at establishing a coherent navigable network in Europe;

-       co-operation in research and the perfecting of equipment for multimodal transport operations and for the handling of containers;

recommend that the States interested in projects of common interest should consider under what conditions it would be possible to establish them, and if they so desire, create the necessary conditions for their actual implementation.

3. Provisions concerning trade and industrial co-operation

Harmonization of standards

The participating States,

Recognizing the development of international harmonization of standards and technical regulations and of international co-operation in the filed of certification as an important means of eliminating technical obstacles to international trade and industrial co-operation, thereby facilitating their development and increasing productivity,

reaffirm their interest to achieve the widest possible international harmonization of standards and technical regulations;

express their readiness to promote international agreements and other appropriate arrangements on acceptance of certificates of conformity with standards and technical regulations;

consider it desirable to increase international co-operation on standardization, in particular by supporting the activities of intergovernmental and other appropriate organizations in this field.

Arbitration

The participating States,

Considering that the prompt and equitable settlement of disputes may arise from commercial transactions relating to goods and services and contracts for industrial co-operation would contribute to expanding and facilitating trade and co-operation.

Considering that arbitration is an appropriate means of settling such disputes,

recommend, where appropriate, to organizations, enterprises and firms in their countries, to include arbitration clauses in commercial contracts and industrial co-operation contracts, or in special agreements;

recommend that the provisions on arbitration should provide for arbitration under a mutually acceptable set of arbitration rules, and permit arbitration in a third country, taking into account existing intergovernmental and other agreements in this field.

Specific bilateral arrangements

The participating States,

Conscious of the need to facilitate trade and to promote the application of new forms of industrial co-operation,

will consider favorably the conclusion, in appropriate cases, of specific bilateral agreements concerning various problems of mutual interest in the fields of commercial exchanges and industrial co-operation, in particular with a view to avoiding double taxation and to facilitation the transfer of profits and the return of the value of the assets invested.

4. Science and technology

The participating States,

Convinced that scientific and technological co-operation constitutes an important contribution to the strengthening of security and co-operation among them, in that it assists the effective solution of problems of common interests and the improvement of the conditions of human life,

Considering that in developing such co-operation, it is important to promote the sharing of information and experience, facilitating the study and transfer of scientific and technological achievements, as well as the access to such achievements on a mutually advantageous basis and in fields of co-operation agreed between interested parties,

Considering that it is for the potential partners, i.e., the competent organizations, institutions, enterprises, scientists and technologists of the participating States to determine the opportunities for mutually beneficial co-operation and to develop its details.

Affirming that such co-operation can be developed and implemented bilaterally and multilaterally at the governmental and non-governmental levels, for example, through intergovernmental and other agreements, international programs, co-operative projects and commercial channels, while utilizing also various forms of contacts, including direct and individual contacts.

Aware of the need to take measures further to improve scientific and technological co-operation between them.

Possibilities for improving co-operation

Recognize that possibilities exist for further improving scientific and technological co-operation, and to this end, express their intention to remove obstacles to such co-operation, in particular though:

-       the improvement of opportunities for the exchange and dissemination of scientific and technological information among the parties interested in scientific and technological research and co-operation including information related to the organization and implementation of such co-operation;

-       the expeditious implementation and improvement in organization, including programs, of international visits of scientists and specialists in connection with exchanges, conferences and co-operation.

-       the wider use of commercial channels and activities for applied scientific and technological research and for the transfer of achievements in this field while providing information on and protection of intellectual and industrial property rights;

Fields of co-operation

Consider that possibilities to expand co-operation exist within the areas given below as examples, noting that it is for potential partners in the participating countries to identify and develop projects and arrangements of mutual interest and benefit:

Agriculture

Research into new methods and technologies for increasing the productivity of crop cultivation and animal husbandry; the application of chemistry to agriculture; the design, construction and utilization of agricultural machinery; technologies of irrigation and other agricultural land improvement works;

Energy

New technologies of production, transport and distribution of energy aimed at improving the use of existing fuels and sources of hydroenergy, as well as research in the field of new energy sources, including nuclear, solar and geothermal energy;

New technologies, rational use of resources

Research on new technologies and equipment designed in particular to reduce energy consumption and to minimize or eliminate waste;

Transport technology

Research on the means of transport and the technology applied to the development and operation of international, national and urban transport networks including container transport as well as transport safety;

Physics

Study of problems in high energy physics and plasma physics; research in the fields of theoretical and experimental nuclear physics;

Chemistry

Research on problems in electrochemistry and the chemistry of polymers, of natural products, and of metals and alloys, as well as the development of improved chemical technology, especially materials processing; practical application of the latest achievements of chemistry to industry, construction and other sectors of the economy;

Meteorology and hydrology

Meteorological and hydrological research, including methods of collection, evaluation and transmission of data and their utilization for weather forecasting and hydrology forecasting;

Oceanography

Oceanographic research, including the study of air/sea interactions;

Seismological research

Study and forecasting of earthquakes and associated geological changes; development and research of technology of seism-resisting constructions;

Research on glaciology, permafrost and problems of life under conditions of cold

Research on glaciology and permafrost; transportation and construction technologies; human adaptation to climatic extremes and changes in the living conditions of indigenous populations;

Computer, communication and information technologies

Development of computers as well as of telecommunications and information systems; technology associated with computers and telecommunications, including their use for management systems, for production processes, for automation, for the study of economic problems, in scientific research and for the collection, processing and dissemination of information;

Space research

Space exploration and the study of the earth's natural resources and the natural environment by remote sensing in particular with the assistance of satellites and rocket-probes;

Medicine and public health

Research on cardiovascular, tumor and virus diseases, molecular biology, neurophysiology; development and testing of new drugs; study of contemporary problems of pediatrics, gerontology and the organization and techniques of medical services;

Environmental research

Research on specific scientific and technological problems related to human environment.

Forms and methods of co-operation

Express their view that scientific and technological co-operation should, in particular, employ the following forms and methods:

- exchange and circulation of books, periodicals and other scientific and technological publications and papers among interested organizations, scientific and technological institutions, enterprises and scientists and technologists, as well as participation in international programs for the abstracting and indexing of publications;

- exchanges and visits as well as other direct contacts and communications among scientists and technologists, on the basis of mutual agreement and other arrangements, for such purposes as consultations, lecturing and conducting research, including the use of laboratories, scientific libraries, and other documentation centers in connection therewith;

- holding of international and national conferences, symposia, seminars, courses and other meetings of a scientific and technological character, which would include the participation of foreign scientists and technologists;

- joint preparation and implementation of programs and projects of mutual interest on the basis of consultation and agreement among all parties concerned, including, where possible and appropriate, exchanges of experience and research results, and correlation of research programs, between scientific and technological research institutions and organizations;

- use of commercial channels and methods for identifying and transferring technological and scientific developments, including the conclusion of mutually beneficial co-operation arrangements between firms and enterprises in fields agreed upon between them and for carrying out, where appropriate, joint research and development programs and projects;

consider it desirable that periodic exchanges of views and information take place on scientific policy, in particular on general problems of orientation and administration of research and the question of a better use of large-scale scientific and experimental equipment on a co-operative basis;

recommend that, in developing co-operation in the field of science and technology, full use be made of existing practices of bilateral and multilateral co-operation, including that of a regional or sub-regional character, together with the forms and methods of co-operation described in this document;

recommend further that more effective utilization be made of the possibilities and capabilities of existing international organizations, intergovernmental and non-governmental, concerned with science and technology, for improving exchanges of information and experience, as well as for developing other forms of co-operation in fields of common interest, for example:

- in the United Nations Economic Commission for Europe, study of possibilities for expanding multilateral co-operation, taking into account models for projects and research used in various international organizations; and for sponsoring conferences, symposia, and study and working groups such as those which would bring together younger scientists in technologies with eminent specialists in their field;

- through their participation in particular international scientific and technological co-operation programs, including those of UNESCO and other international organizations, pursuit of continuing progress towards the objectives of such programs, notably those of UNISIST with particular respect to information policy guidance, technical advice, information contributions and data processing.

5. Environment

The participating States,

Affirming that the protection and improvement of the environment, as well as the protection of nature and the rational utilization of its resources in the interests of present and future generations, is one of the tasks of major importance to the well-being of peoples and the economic development of all countries and that many environmental problems, particularly in Europe, can be solved effectively only through close international co-operation.

Acknowledging that each of the participating States, in accordance with the principles of international law, ought to ensure, in a spirit of co-operation, that activities carried out on its territory do not cause degradation of the environment in another State or in areas lying beyond the limits of national jurisdiction.

Considering that the success of any environmental policy presupposes that all population groups and social forces, aware of their responsibilities, help to protect and improve the environment, which necessitates continued and thorough educative action, particularly with regard to youth.

Affirming that experience has shown that economic development and technological progress must be compatible with the protection of the environment and the preservation of historical and cultural values; that damage to the environment is best avoided by preventive measures; and that the ecological balance must be preserved in the exploitation and management of natural resources.

Aims of co-operation

Agree to the following aims of co-operation, in particular:

\- to study, with a view to their solution, those environmental problems which, by their nature, are of a multilateral, bilateral, regional or sub-regional dimension; as well as to encourage the development of an interdisciplinary approach to environmental problems:

\- to increase the effectiveness of national and international measures for the protection of the environment by the comparison and, if appropriate, the harmonization of methods of gathering and analyzing facts, by improving the knowledge of pollution phenomena and rational utilization of natural resources, by the exchange of information, by the harmonization of definitions and the adoption, as far as possible, of a common terminology in the field of the environment;

\- to take the necessary measures to bring environmental policies closer together and, where appropriate and possible, to harmonize them;

\- to encourage, where possible and appropriate, national and international efforts by their interested organizations, enterprises and firms in the development, production and improvement of equipment designed for monitoring, protection and enhancing the environment.

Fields of co-operation

To attain these aims, the participating States will make use of every suitable opportunity to co-operate in the field of environment and, in particular, within the areas described below as examples:

Control of air pollution

Desulphurization of fossil fuels and exhaust gases; pollution control of heavy metals, particles, aerosols, nitrogen oxides, in particular those emitted by transport, power stations, and other industrial plants; systems and methods of observation and control of air pollution and its effects, including long-range transport of air pollutants;

Water pollution control and fresh water utilization

Prevention and control of water pollution, in particular of transboundary rivers and international lakes; techniques for the improvement of the quality of water and further development of ways and means for industrial and municipal sewage effluent purification; methods of assessment of fresh water resources and the improvement of their utilization, in particular by developing methods of production which are less polluting and lead to less consumption of fresh water;

Protection of the marine environment

Protection of the marine environment of participating States, and especially the Mediterranean Sea, from pollutants emanating from land-based sources and those from ships and other vessels, notably the harmful substances listed in Annexes I and II to the London Convention on the Prevention of Marine Pollution by the Dumping of Wastes and Other Matters; problems of maintaining marine ecological balances and food chains, in particular such problems as may arise from the exploration and exploitation of biological and mineral resources of the seas and the sea-bed;

Land utilization and soils

Problems associated with more effective use of lands, including land amelioration, reclamation and recultivation: control of soil pollution, water and air erosion, as well as other forms of soil degradation; maintaining and increasing the productivity of soils with due regard for the possible negative effects of the application of chemical fertilizers and pesticides;

Nature conservation and nature reserves

Protection of nature and nature reserves; conservation and maintenance of existing genetic resources, especially rare animal and plant species; conservation of natural ecological systems; establishment of nature reserves and other protected landscapes and areas, including their use for research, tourism, recreation and other purposes;

Improvement of environmental conditions in areas of human settlement

Environmental conditions associated with transport, housing, working areas, urban development and planning, water supply and sewage disposal systems; assessment of harmful effects of noise, and noise control methods; collection, treatment and utilization of wastes, including the recovery and recycling of materials; research on substitutes for non-biodegradable substances;

Fundamental research, monitoring, forecasting and assessment of environmental changes

Study of changes in climate, landscapes and ecological balances under the impact of both natural factors and human activities; forecasting of possible generic changes in flora and fauna as a result of environmental pollution; harmonization of statistical data, development of scientific concepts and systems of monitoring networks, standardized methods of observation, measurement and assessment of changes in the biosphere; assessment of the effects of environmental pollution levels and degradation of the environment upon human health; study and development of criteria and standards for various environmental pollutants and regulation regarding production and use of various products;

Legal and administrative measures

Legal and administrative measures for the protection of the environment including procedures for establishing environmental impact assessments.

Forms and methods of co-operation

The participating States declare that problems relating to the protection and improvement of the environment will be solved on both a bilateral and a multilateral, including regional and sub-regional, basis, making full use of existing patterns and forms of co-operation. They will develop co-operation in the field of the environment in particular by taking into consideration the Stockholm Declaration on the Human Environment, relevant resolutions of the United Nations General Assembly and the United Nations Economic Commission for Europe Prague symposium on environmental problems.

The participating States are resolved that co-operation in the field of the environment will be implemented in particular through;

-       exchanges of scientific and technical information, documentation and research results, including information on the means of determining the possible effects on the environment of technical and economic activities;

-       organization of conferences, symposia and meetings of experts;

-       exchanges of scientists, specialists and trainees;

-       joint preparation and implementation of programs and projects for the study and solution of various problems of environmental protection;

-       harmonization, where appropriate and necessary, of environmental protection standards and norms, in particular with the object of avoiding possible difficulties in trade which may arise from efforts to resolve ecological problems of production process and which relate to the achievement of certain environmental qualities in manufactured products;

-       consultations on various aspects of environmental protection,   as agreed upon among countries concerned,   especially in connection with problems which could have international consequences.

The participating States will further develop such co-operation by:

-       promoting the progressive development,   codification and implementation of international law as one means of preserving and enhancing the human environment, including principles and practices, as accepted by them,   relating to pollution and other environmental damage caused by activities within the jurisdiction or control of their States affecting other countries and regions;

-       supporting and promoting the implementation of relevant international Conventions to which they are parties, in particular those designed to prevent and combat marine and fresh water pollution, recommending States to ratify Conventions which have already been singed,   as well as considering possibilities of accepting other appropriate Conventions to which they are not parties at present;

-       advocating the inclusion,   where appropriate and possible,   of the various areas of co-operation into the programs of work of the United Nations Economic Commission for Europe, supporting such co-operation within the framework of the Commission and of the United Nations Environment Program,   and taking into account he work of other competent international organizations of which they are members;

-       making wider use,   in all types of co-operation,   of information already available from national and international sources,   including internationally agreed criteria,   and utilizing the possibilities and capabilities of various competent international organizations.

The participating States agree on the following recommendations on specific measures:

-       to develop through international co-operation an extensive program for the monitoring and evaluation of the long-range transport of air pollutants, starting with sulfur dioxide and with possible extension to other pollutants, and to this end to take into account basic elements of a co-operation program which were identified by the experts who met in Oslo in December 1974 at the invitation of the Norwegian Institute of Air Research:

-       to advocate that within the framework of the United Nations Economic Commission for Europe a study be carried out of procedures and relevant experience relating to the activities of Governments in developing the capabilities of their countries to predict adequately environmental consequences of economic activities and technological development.

BIBLIOGRAPHY

BIBLIOGRAPHY AND NOTES

Abreu, Juan: "La Madre," Diario Las Americas, December 19, 1993.

Adelman, Ken: "The Russian Economic Reform: A Lot of Noise and Few Nuts," Diario Las Americas, Miami, March 9, 1988.

Aguilar Leon, Dr. Luis: "Cuba: The Endless Struggle," Diario Las Americas, Miami, March 13, 1988.

Aguirre, Dr. Horacio: "Democracy and Freedom," conferences and an editorial in Diario Las Americas, 1985.

Alonso Avila, Dr. Antonio: "History of the Cuban Communist Party," 1969

Alvarado, Dr. Adalberto: "Marti's Thoughts," Gonzalez Printing, Miami, 1985.

American Convention on Human Rights, November, 1969.

American Declaration of the Rights and Duties of Man, April, 1948.

American International Conferences, 1889-1936. Preface by Leo S. Rowe and Introduction by James Brown Scott, Washington, D.C. Carnegie Endowment for International Peace, 1938.

Amnesty International, London. Several reports on the status of human rights in Cuba, 1986 and 1987.

Arboleya, Dr. Carlos J: "Economy and Progress," 1987.

Arciniegs, Dr. German: "Why Castille?" Alas, Bogota, Colombia. Diario Las Americas, Miami, October 15, 1987.

Ardura, Dr. Ernesto: "The Americas on the Horizon," Salvat Editorial House, Miami, 1984.

Arenas, Reinaldo: "The Necessity for Freedom," Kosmos Editorial, Inc., 1976.

Arredondo, Dr. Alberto: "Agrarian Reform: The Cuban Experience," San Juan Editorial House, Puerto Rico, 1969.

Basic Instruments of the Organization of American States. 1970.

Baquero, Eng. Gaston: "Cuba, Liberty and Culture," Spain, 1990.

Bauta, Dr. Guillermo: "The Benedi Doctrine," Diario El Norte, Chicago, October 21, 1987.

Benedi Doctrine: Approved by unanimous consent of the United States Senate to be printed in the Senate Congressional Record, August 2, 1989.

Benedi, Dr. Claudio F.: "Confrontation between Anthropocentrism and Theocentrism." Several documents submitted to the Organization of American States in the Ordinary General Assemblies.

Benedi, Dr. Claudio F.: "Institutional Violation of Human Rights," Congressional Record (Senate) 1986.

Benedi, Dr. Claudio F.: "Institutional Violation of Human Rights." Twenty-Seven documents of appearances before the Inter-American Commission on Human Rights of the OAS, submitted over two decades, 1961 - 1993.

Benedi, Dr. Claudio F.: "The Foresight of Felix Varela," Americas, OAS, Washington, D.C., April, 1977 (in English, Spanish and Portuguese).

Botifoll, Dr. Luis: "The Banking System of Cuba," 1980.

Bravo Lira, Dr. Bernardino: "What was the Independence?," El Mercurio, Santiago de Chile, September 20, 1987.

Brodski, Joseph (Nobel Prize winner): "The Ignored Continent of Russian Literature," published by Dr. Rafael Gomez, El Mercurio, Santiago de Chile, December 6, 1987.

Brouwer, Dr. Emilio A.: "Liberty and Democracy," declaration and document, Association of Cuban University Professionals, Washington, D.C., 1962.

Bush, Hon. George, President of the United States: "A Document on the Institutional Violation of Human Rights by Dr. Claudio F. Benedi," 1988.

Bush, Hon. George, President of the United States: "In a thoughtful and powerful fashion, Dr. Benedi has documented the systematic violation of human rights by the Cuban government and other communist regimes, and has encouraged the international community to oppose these assaults on human freedom and dignity. We owe him a great debt.," The White House, Washington, D.C., 1989.

Bustamante Sirven, Dr. Antonio: "Public and Private International Law," 1942.

Cabrera Leyva, Dr. Guillermo: "The Meaning of the Holy Week," Diario Las Americas, Miami, March 26, 1988.

Capo, Dr. Moravia and Felipe Gonzalez: "Human Rights Declaration: Commission on Human Rights of Cuban Municipalities in Exile, 1993.

Carbonell-Cortina, Dr. Nestor: "Cuba: Resist and Await," booklet, 1993.

Carreno, Jose: "Fifty Testimonies from Cuban Political Prisoners," a publication of the Cuban Historical Prisoners Association, Miami, 1987.

Carrillo, Dr. Justo: "Cuba 1933 (Students, Yankees and Soldiers)," published by the Inter-American Studies Institute, University of Miami, 1985.

Castellanos, Lic. Andres: "The Issue of Human Rights," in process.

Charter of the Organization of American States, OAS Documents, 1948- 1993.

Charter of the United Nations and Statutes of the International Court of Justice, published by the United Nations, Office of Public Information, New York, June, 1961.

Clark, Dr. Juan: "Religious Repression in Cuba," University of Miami, Institute for Inter-American Studies, Coral Gables, Florida, 1986.

Clavijo, Dr. Uva: "The Challenges of 'Golden Letters'," Diario Las Americas, Miami, March 25, 1988.

Clinton, Mr. William J., President of the United States of America: Speech before the United Nations General Assembly, on September 27, 1993: "...Human Rights are not something conditional, bounded by culture, but rather universal, granted by God."

Constitution of the Republic of Cuba, 1940. Cuban Civil Laws and their Jurisprudence, Vol. I, by Dr. Mariano Sanchez Roca, Editorial Lex, Havana, 1951.

Conte Aguero, Dr. Luis: "Cuba in my Heart," Hialeah, Fl., 1993.

Costa, Dr. Octavio R. : "Variations about God, Time, Death and Other Issues," Los Angeles, California, 1987.

Creasy, Sir Edward: "The Rise and Progress of the English Constitution," London, 1980.

Cuba Socialist Constitutions, published in the Official Cuba Gazette on February 24, 1976 and August 1, 1992.

Cuban Episcopei: "Pastoral Letter," September 8, 1993.

Cubenas, Dr. Jose A.: "Ruben Dario: A Restorer of the Conscience of the World Harmony," 1975.

De La Fe, Ernesto: "Forbidden to Think."

De Las Casas, Fr. Bartolome: "Very Breif Account of the Destruction of the Indies," 1552.

De Oliveira, Prof. Plinio Correa: "Nobility and Traditional Analogous Elites in the Allocutions of Pius XII- A Theme Illuminating American Social History," 1993.

De Oliveira, Dr. Plinio Correa: "Representative Regime and Chronic Ignorance," Diario Las Americas, Miami, March 2, 1988.

De Vitoria, Father Francisco: "De Indis et de Jure Belli Relection," Carnegie Institute, Washington, D.C., 1917.

Declaration of Independence of the United States of America, 1776.

Del Valle, Msgr. Raul: Prologue to the Second Edition of "Felix Varela, Torch Bearer from Cuba," by Joseph and Helen M. McCadden, San Juan, Puerto Rico, 1984.

Deniau, Jean Francois: "Resistance Movements," Kosmos Editorial, Inc., 1988.

Diaz-Balart, Dr. Lincoln: "Synthesis of a Conference: Cuba in Transition," Diario Las Americas, December 2, 1993.

Diaz Verson, Dr. Salvador: Investigated and discovered that Fidel Castro was a Communist since he was a young man, and a member of a Secret Soviet Cell, ID # 583.

Docht, Alfonso: "Economic and Social Foundations of European Culture," Fondo de Cultura Economica, Mexico, 1936.

Document-Program: "The Inter-American System, The Organization of American States and Cuba," presented by Dr. Benedi to the Twenty-Third Ordinary Period of Sessions of the General Assembly of the Organization of American States (OAS) on June 7, 1993, and signed by Dr. Roberto Rodriguez de Aragon and Dr. Claudio F. Benedi-Beruff.

Duarte Oropesa, Dr. Jose: "Historiography of Cuba," 1993.

Errazuriz McKenna, Dr. Carlos J.: "The Pure Theory of Law: A Critical Overview," Navarra University Editions, Inc., Pamploma, Spain, 1986.

Estorino, Julio: "Song to Cuba," poem published in Diario Las Americas, 1991.

Fernandez, Mr. Esteban: "Between the Mother and the Fatherland," newspaper The 20th of May, Los Angeles, California, December 11, 1993.

Fernandez Caubi, Dr. Luis: "All Satellites are by Force," Diario Las Americas, Miami, March 26, 1988.

Fernandez Escobio, Dr. Fernando: "Cuban Roots."

Fibla, Dr. Alberto: "El 84," 1993.

Galan Pino, Sergio: "The Peruvian Embassy: A Jump Towards Freedom, Twin Printing, Miami.

Garcia Tuduri, Dr. Mercedes: "The Philosophic Thought in Cuba."

Geyer, Georgie Anne: "The Latins," Doubleday & Co., Inc., New York, 1970.

Geyer, Georgie Anne: Why we Ridicule the Exceptional Person," Diario Las Americas, March 2, 1988.

Gil, Cesareo: "Political Mission of the Church," Editorial Tripode, Venezuela, 1978.

Glucksmann, Andre: "Descartes, the Adventurer," Publishing by Flammarion, France.

Gonzalez, Rev. Dr. Pastor: "Father Felix Varela: Theology and Education," Saint Charles Seminary, Cuba, 1976.

Grau Alsina, Dr. Ramon: "The Institutional Violation of Human Rights (Benedi Doctrine)," documented before the United Nations

Commission on Human Rights in Geneva, March 1987, in writing and orally.

Grocio, Hugo: "De Jure Belli ac Deo Legislatore," several editions.

Guerra Sanchez, Dr. Ramiro: "The Ten-Year War," Editorial Ciencias Sociales, Havana, 1972.

Guevara, Miguel, and Diaz, Santiago: "Death Wears a Green Dress," Revista Ideal, Miami, 1982.

Gutierrez Khan, Dr. Asela: "Cuba and its Destiny," 1992.

Helsinki Accords, 1975, contained in the Acts of the Conference on Security and Cooperation in Europe, which in its Seventh Clause refers to respect for human rights and basic freedoms, including those of thought, conscience, religion and beliefs, signed by 35 nations, including the U.S. and the U.S.S.R.

Hernandez Travieso, Dr. Antonio: "Father Varela: A Biography of the Forger of the Cuban Conscience," Ediciones Universal, Miami, 1986.

Hispanic-American Center for Juridical Studies: "The Inter-American System," a study on its development and strengthening, Instituto de Cultura Hispanica, Madrid, 1966.

Hoffman, Dr. Oscar E.: "The Mystery of the Century," Ediciones Tiempo de Cultura, Buenos Aires, 1984.

Huertas, Dr. Enrique: Declarations and Conclusions of the "Colegio Medico Cubano Libre" and the XII International Congress, Diario Las Americas, July 4, 1993.

Ibanez Langlois, Dr. J. Miguel: "State, Conscience and Democracy," Mercurio newspaper, Santiago de Chile, 1987.

Illan, Dr. Jose M.: "Cuba, Notes of an Economy in Ruins," Miami, 1964.

Inter-American Commission on Human Rights, Annual Reports, 1985-86 and 1986-87, and 1989-90.

Inter-American Commission on Human Rights, OAS: Seven reports on the status of Human Rights in Cuba, 1962-1983.

Inter-American Commission on Human Rights, Seventh Report, October, 1983. It deals with the Institutional Violation of Human Rights and the Violation in its Human Dimension, denounced by Dr. Claudio Benedi in several appearances.

International Texts on Human Rights, EUNSA, Pamplona, Spain, 1978.

Jorge, Dr. Antonio: "Cuba, Economics and Politics," interviews, articles and Essays, 1991-1993.

Jorge, Dr. Guillermo J.: "The Benedi Doctrine," Miami, January 8, 1988.

Jorge, Dr. Guillermo J.: "The Future of Democracy in the New Cuba," booklet, 1993.

Kelsen, Hans: "Essence and Value of Democracy," 1938.

Kelsen, Hans: "Subjective Law," University of La Habana, Cuba, 1939.

Kintner, William R.: "Soviet Global Strategy," Hero Books, Fairfax, Va., 1987.

Kirkpatrick, Dr. Jeanne: :The Book by the Kennedy Economist Excessively Simplifies those Factors the Intervene in the Ascent and Fall of Nations," Diario Las Americas, March 6, 1988.

Kissinger, Dr. Henry: "My Memories," 1992.

Lapp, Ignace: "From Karl Marx to Jesus Christ," Sheed & Ward, New York, 1958.

Larrabee, Eric: "A Panorama of the U.S. Culture," Editorial Sur,

Buenos Aires, 1958.

Lavin, Dr. Pablo F.: "Juan Bautista Alberti, a Pioneer," Diario Las Americas, Miami, 1985.

Law of the Penal Code (Law No. 21), February 15, 1979, Official Gazette, March 1, 1979, Havana, Cuba.

Law for the Organization of the Judiciary System (Law No. 4), Offial Gazette, August 25, 1977, Havana, Cuba.

Lazo, Dr. Mario: "American Policy Failures in Cuba: Dagger in the Heart," Twin Circle Publishing Co., New York, 1968.

Liddy, G. Gordon: "Will," St. Martin's Press, New York City, NY., 1980.

Limbaugh, Rush: "See, I Told You So," Simon & Schuster, New York, 1993.

Lippe, Stuart: "Resolution on Human Rights," 1991.

Manach, Dr. Jorge: "Marti's Spirit," Editorial San Juan, Puerto Rico, 1973.

Manach, Dr. Jorge: "Marti, the Apostle," Editorial Cultural, Havana, Cuba, 1932.

Manalich, Dr. Ovidio M.: "For the Theory of the Cuban Case," about the evolution of the revolution, Diario Las Americas, October 15, 1987.

Manrara, Dr. Luis V.: "The Truth About Cuba," declaration, 1964.

Manual of Dispositions in Force in the Matter of Human RIghts in the Inter-American System. Secretariat General of the Organization of American States, 1985.

Marinas, Dr. Manuel J.: "I Accuse," a book published by the Association of Cuban Attorneys in Exile and the Fraternity of Attorneys Graduated in 1942.

Mario, Mr. Luis: "A Song to Cuba," poetry. "Cuba in My Poems," book, 1993.

Marquez Sterling, Dr. Carlos: "History of Cuba: From Colon to Castro," Las Americas Publishing Co., New York City, 1963.

Marquez Sterling, Dr. Manuel: "The Cauto Runs Deeply," 1992.

Marrero, Dr. Levi: "Cuba: Economy and Society," several volumes. Editorial Playor, Puerto Rico, 1971-1993.

Martinez Marquez, Dr. Guillermo: "Benedi before the Inter-American Commission on Human Rights," Diario Las Americas, Miami, September 10, 1986.

Martinez Saenz, Dr. Joaquin: "Marti, the Sublime Unadapted," Congress of Cuba, 1951.

Martinez Saenz, Dr. Joaquin: "The Economic Development of Cuba," 1959.

Marx, Karl: "Das Kapital," Editorial Cultura, 1936.

Marx, Karl, and Engels, Frederick: "Manifesto of the Communist Party," Editorial Progresso, 1979.

Mederos, Dr. Elena, **Benedi,** Dr. Claudio F. and **Calzon**, Frank: "Human Rights in Cuba," magazine, 1975.

Medrano, Dr. Humberto: "El Presidio Politico en Cuba," Miami, 1967.

Mejia Gonzales, Dr. Luis: "Nicaragua, a Martyr," Diario Las Americas, 1992.

Menedez Pelayo, Dr. Marcelino: "Studies and Discourses of Historicle and Literary Critique," Superior Council for Scientific Investigations, 1941, Aldus, Corp. of Graphic Arts, Santander, Spain, Volumes I through IV.

Mesa Lago, Dr. Carmelo: "Dialetics of the Cuban Revolution: From Carismatic Idealism to Institutional Pragmatism," Editorial Playor, Spain.

Mijares, Dr. Jose A.: "A Project for the Complete Reconstruction of Cuba," Tampa, Fl., 1961, 1987 and 1993 (Third Edition).

Montaner, Dr. Carlos A.: "Snapshots on the Edge of Abyss," Editorial San Juan, Puerto Rico.

Montiel, Dr. Francisco F.: "The Three Wars of Communism," Diario Las Americas, March 2, 1988.

Mora Morales, Esther Pilar: "Female Political Prisoners in Castroite Cuba," Published by Revista Ideal, Miami, 1986.

Novak, Michael: On Pope John Paul II's Encyclical, "The Splendor of the Truth," article in The Washington Times, October 24, 1993.

Novak, Robert: "Religion, State & Society," several journalistic works, Washington, D.C.

Oliva, Major General Erneido A.: (Second in command of the Bay of Pigs Invasion), declarations in April 1961 in Cuba, IBEAMERICA (magazine) July 15, 1989, and Diario Las Americas, Miami, 1992.

Ortega, Luis: "The Dream and the Distance," Ediciones Ganivet, Mexico, 1968.

Ortega Gasset, Jose: "What Values Are," Editorial Revista Occidente, Madrid, Spain.

Osvaldo, Don Julio: "Purunga," Editora Corripio, Dominican Republic, 1986.

Otero Dalman, Dr. Antonio: "Years of Lies Under Soviet Imperialism," Editorial A.I.P., 1976.

Pellecer, Carlos M.: "Useful after Death," B. Costa-MIC, Editor, Mexico, 1967.

Perera, Dr. Hilda: "Plantado," Talleres Graficos Duplex, Inc., Spain, 1981.

Perera, Dr. Ana Maria: "The Women in the Cultural, Educational and Social Development."

Perez, Demetrio, Jr.: "America Dorada," Lincoln-Marti Schools, 1994.

Perez, Roberto M.: "Benedi Doctrine on the Institutional Violation of Human Rights," a statement, Diario Las Americas, July 14, 1987.

Perez-Roura, Armando: "Towards Democracy in Cuba," Toma Notas, Radio Mambi, Miami, Florida, 1993.

Permuy, Jesus: "Human Rights Institutional Violations: Benedi Doctrine," document presented by the Christian Democrat before the United Nations, Geneva, February, 1989.

Pope John Paul II: "Encyclical: Veritatis Splendor (Splendor of the Truth)," October, 1993.

Pope John Paul II: "Sollicitud Rei Socialis," an Encyclical, December 30, 1987.

Portell Villa, Dr. Herminio: "A Question of Human Rights," Diario Las Americas, Miami, October 4, 1986.

Portell Vila, Dr. Hermino: "Justice Must Be Done," Diario Las Americas, June 10, 1986.

Portell Vila, Dr. Hermino: "Narciso Lopez and his Time."

Portell Vila, Dr. Herminio: "New History of the Republic of Cuba," La Moderna Poesia, Miami, 1986.

Protocol of the Charter of the Organization of American States, 1967.

Ramos, Dr. Marcos A.: "A Panorama of Protestantism in Cuba," Editorial Caribe, 1986.

Ramos Avello, Dr. Oscar: "Cuba, Unredeemed," Diario Las Americas, Miami, November 10, 1989.

Rangel, Carlos: "From the Good Savage to the Good Revolutionary," Kosmos Editorial, Inc., 1976.

Rasco, Dr. Jose I.: "Communism is Dead," Diario Las Americas, March 23, 1988.

Ravines, Eudocio: "The Great Swindle," Lectorum Corp., 1974.

Reagan, Hon. Ronald, President of the United States: Public letter dated April 30, 1987, "The Institutional suppression of Human Rights in Cuba has been carefully documented by the respected human rights activist, Dr. Claudio Benedi."

Reagan, Hon. Ronald, President of the United States: Speech in October, 1986, in which he denounced the Institutional Violation of Human Rights in the Soviet Union before the Secretary General of the USSR in Iceland.

Regalado, Tomas P.: "Dr. Benedi before the Inter-American Commission on Human Rights of the OAS," The Miami Herald, February 25, 1986.

Regalado, Tomas P.: "The Return to Democracy and Liberty in Cuba is Inevitable," Radio Mambi, Miami, Florida, 1993.

Regulations of the Inter-American Commission on Human Rights, March 7, 1985.

Remos, Dr. Ariel: "Dialogue and the Democratic Left," Diario Las Americas, Miami, December 6, 1993.

Remos, Dr. Ariel: "Dr. Benedi Urges the OAS to Speed Up the Eighth Report," 1985.

Remos, Dr. Ariel: "Why Communism is Ahead of Us," Diario Las Americas, Miami, March 22,, 1988.

Revel, Jean Francois: "How Democracies Perish, Editorial Planeta, Spain, 1988, and Doubleday & Co., Inc., Garden City, N.Y., 1984.

Reyes, Dr. Manuel J.: "A New Cuba," Diario Las Americas, Miami, November 4, 1987.

Riano Jauma, Dr. Ricardo: "Claudio Benedi, an Exponent of our Generation." Diario Las Americas, December 18, 1986.

Ribo, Luis S.: "Message to Cuba," El Mambi, Tampa, Fl., 1993.

Roa, Dr. Arsenio: "The Five Century of America Discover: Projection-Actuality," conference, 1993.

Rodon, Dr. Lincoln: "My 60 Years of Public Life," Miami, 1992.

Rodriguez Cepero, Dr. Luis (Chairman of the Cuban National Association of Attorneys): "The Cuban Constitution," Miami, 1991.

Ros-Lehtinen, Ileana: "The Law of the Cuban Democracy," Diario Las Americas, December 12, 1993.

Rosete, Hada: "The Benedi Doctrine," a denunciation before the Organization of American States about the Institutional Violation of Human Rights in Cuba, presented by Dr. Claudio F. Benedi. "Noticias del Mundo," New York City, March 29, 1985.

Rostovtseff, M.: "Economic & Social History of the Roman Empire," Editorial Aguilar, Madrid, Spain.

Sakharov, Andrei, and Boner, Yelena: "A Project for a Soviet Constitution: Human Rights in the Soviet Union."

Sanchez Boudy, Dr. Jose: "Cuba: Present and Future."

Sanchez Boudy, Dr. Jose: "The Cuban Process," essays and articles, 1987-1993.

Sanchez de Bustamante Sirven, Dr. Antonio: "Public and Private International Law," 1942.

Santa Teresa, Father Silverio de: "St. John of the Cross," Third Edition, Burgos, Spain, 1963. Mount Carmel Tipographic Works.

Santovenia, Dr. Emeterio S., and Shelton, Dr. Raul M.: "Cuba and Its History," Rema Press, 1965.

Schumpeter, Joseph: "Theory of Economic Development," Fondo de Cultura Economica, Mexico.

Sciacca, Michele F.: "Plato," Editorial Troquel, Inc., Buenos Aires, 1959.

Second Vatican Council, Constitutions, Decrees, Statements. Library of Christian Authors, Madrid, 1967. Editorial Catolica, S.A., Madrid, Spain, 1965.

Segura Bustamante, Dr. Ines: "Cuba, the 20th. Century and the 1930 Generation," Ediciones Universal, Miami, 1986.

Shifter, Richard: "The Soviet Constitution: Myth and Reality," U.S. Department of State, Bureau of Public Affairs, Washington, D.C., 1987.

Smith, Adam: "The Wealth of Nations," Fondo de Cultura Economica, Mexico.

Solzhenitsyn, Alexander I.: "The Gulag Archipelago, 1918-1956," Harper & Row, New York City, 1976.

Spaeman, Dr. Robert: "What is Progress?" El Mercurio Newspaper, Santiago de Chile, November 29, 1987.

Statutes of the Inter-American Commission for Human Rights, October, 1979.

Statutes of the Inter-American Court for Human Rights, October, 1979.

Suarez, Father Francisco: "The Legibus ac Deo Legislatore," Spain.

Symms, Senator Steve: "Resolution Cuba-Symms," approved by 77 senators in 1984, published in the Congressional Record, 1984. (Joint resolution).

Tamargo, Agustin: "Cuba, the Price of Freedom," and article, The Miami Herald, 1985.

The Inter-American Convention on Human Rights, a publication of the General Secretariat of the OAS, Inter-American Commission on Human Rights, 1980.

The Jerusalem Bible.

The Koran.

The Talmud.

Torre, Angel de la: "Dr. Claudio F. Benedi: Adalid de la Juridicidad Hemisferica y Diacono Filial de la Diaspora Cubana," New York, January 21, 1985.

Torrente-Iglesias, Aurelio: "Dream of a 20 of May," Diario Las Americas, May 20, 1993.

Torricelli, Robert: The Cuban Democracy Act: Law H.R. 4168. (With the participaction and support of Jorge Mas Canosa).

Toutain, J.C.: "The Economy in the Ancient World," Editorial Gonzalez Porto, Mexico, 1967.

Travieso-Diaz, Dr. Matias: "Cuban Transition Project," Law Offices of Shaw, Pittman, Potts and Trowbridge, 1993.

United Nations Commission on Human Rights. UNO's publications, 1989-1993.

Universal Declaration of Human Rights, December, 1948.

Uslar Pietri, Dr. Arturo: "Twenty Years Ago," Diario Las Americas, Miami, March 9, 1988.

Valladares, Armando: "From My Wheelchair," Interbooks Corp., Coral Gables, Fl., 1976.

Valle, Msgr. Raul del: "Felix Varela: A Forger of the Fatherland," a conference, 1983.

Valls, Jose: "Where I Am, There is no Light and There are Bars," written in Cuba. Editorial Playor, 1981.

Varela, Father Felix: "Remarks on the Political Constitution of the Spanish Monarchy," Library of Cuban Authhors, Volume VIII.

Vargas Gomez, Dr. Andres: "...what Dr. Claudio Benedi calls 'Institutional Violation of Human Rights'," a statement published in Diario Las Americas, Miami, January 26, 1985.

Varona, Dr. Alberto J.: "Francisco Bilbao, a Revolutionary of the Americas," Editorial Troquel, Buenos Aires.

Varona, Dr. Manuel Antonio de: "Freedom and Democracy," a document, 1985.

Vega Ceballos, Victor: "Benedi and Human Rights," Diario Las Americas, Miami, 1991.

Weber, Max: "Economy and Society," Fondo de Cultura Economica, Mexico.

Wheeler, John Archibald: "The Quantum Revolution."

Zamora, Antonio: "American Constitutional Digest," Editorial Claridad, First Edition, September, 1958.

Zayas-Bazan Perdomo, Dr. Hector: "The Benedi Doctrine," a booklet from the Cuban Patriotic Board, California, 1989.

Zayas-Bazan Perdomo, Dr. Hector: "Trajectory of the Pharmacy in Cuba: The Socialist Ideas Expropriation and Deterioration of a Profession," (Institutional Violation of the Human Rights), Conference, October 26-30, 1993, Costa Rica, C.A.

Zendegui, Dr. Guillermo de: "El Apostolado de Claudio Benedi," Diario Las Americas, Miami, October 10, 1992.

Zendegui, Dr. Guillermo de: "En la Carta de la O.N.U. no estan todos los Derechos Humanos," recognized first by Dr. Benedi, Diario Las Americas, Miami, October 30, 1993.

Zendegui, Dr. Guillermo de: "We are all Guilty," 1992.